# EVERYTHING YOU NEED TO KNOW ABOUT

# ENGLISH
## HOMEWORK

### ANNE ZEMAN
### KATE KELLY

AN IRVING PLACE PRESS BOOK

SCHOLASTIC
REFERENCE

Cover design, Red Herring Design; Cover illustration, Sarajo Frieden
Interior design, Bennett Gewirtz, Gewirtz Graphics, Inc.; Interior illustration, Greg Paprocki

Library of Congress Cataloging-in-Publication Data


Zeman, Anne
    Everything you need to know about English homework / Anne Zeman
      and Kate Kelly.
          p.   cm. — (Scholastic homework reference series)
    Includes index.
    1. Language arts—Juvenile literature. 2. Homework—Juvenile literature.
    [1. Language arts. 2. Homework.] I. Kelly, Kate. II. Title.
    III. Series: Scholastic homework reference series.
    LB1576.Z46  1994
    372.6—dc20
    ISBN  0-439-62545-9
    AC                                                          93-46358
                                                                  CIP


10  9  8  7  6  5                                              08  09

Printed in the U.S.A.
First Printing this Edition, January 2005

# Contents

# Part 4. Parts of Speech

# Part 5. Writing Tools

# Part 6. Creative Writing

# Part 7. Practical Writing

# Part 8. Reading

# Introduction

It's homework time—but you have questions. You need some help, but no adults are around, and you can't reach your classmates on the phone. Where can you go for help?

## What Questions Does This Book Answer?

In *Everything You Need to Know About English Homework*, you will find a wealth of information, including the answers to some of the most commonly asked English homework questions.

- What are homonyms, homophones, and antonyms? Homonyms, homophones, and homographs are defined on page 27. A table of homonyms appears on pages 28–30. Antonyms are the subject of page 36.

- How do you use a dictionary to find the meaning of a word? A guide to using a dictionary is found on pages 34–38.

- How do you write a book report? A feature on book reports is found on page 108.

- How do you find the main idea? The main idea of a paragraph is defined and illustrated on pages 66–67.

- When and how do you use quotation marks? The proper use of quotation marks and other common punctuation marks is listed on pages 60–64.

- How do you spell *exaggerate* and other difficult words? Commonly misspelled words are the subject of a table on page 27.

- How do you  write a poem? Guidelines for writing poems are found on page 91.

- Where do you put an apostrophe to show possession? Find out how apostrophes are used to show possession on page 60.

- What is the difference between a simile and a metaphor? Metaphor and simile are defined on pages 80 and 82.

- How do you form contractions? Contractions are defined and illustrated on page 33.

# What Is the *Everything You Need to Know About...Homework* series?

The *Everything You Need to Know About...Homework* series is a set of unique reference resources written especially to answer the homework questions of fourth-, fifth-, and sixth-graders. The series provides ready information to answer commonly asked homework questions in a variety of subjects. Here you'll find facts, charts, definitions, and explanations, complete with examples and illustrations that will supplement schoolwork colorfully, clearly, and comprehensively.

# A Note to Parents

It's important to support your children's efforts to do homework. Welcome their questions and see that they are equipped with a well-lighted desk or table, pencils, paper, and any other books or equipment that they need—such as rulers, calculators, reference books or textbooks, and so on. You might also set aside a special time each day for doing homework, a time when you're available to answer questions that may arise. But don't do your children's homework for them. Remember, homework should create a bond between school and home. It is meant to enhance the lessons taught at school on a daily basis, and to promote good work and study habits. Although it is gratifying to have your children present flawless homework papers, the flawlessness should be a result of your children's explorations and efforts—not your own.

The *Everything You Need to Know About...Homework* series is designed to help your children complete their homework on their own to the best of their abilities. If they're stuck, you can use these books with them to help find answers to troubling homework problems. And remember, when the work is done, praise your children for a job well done.

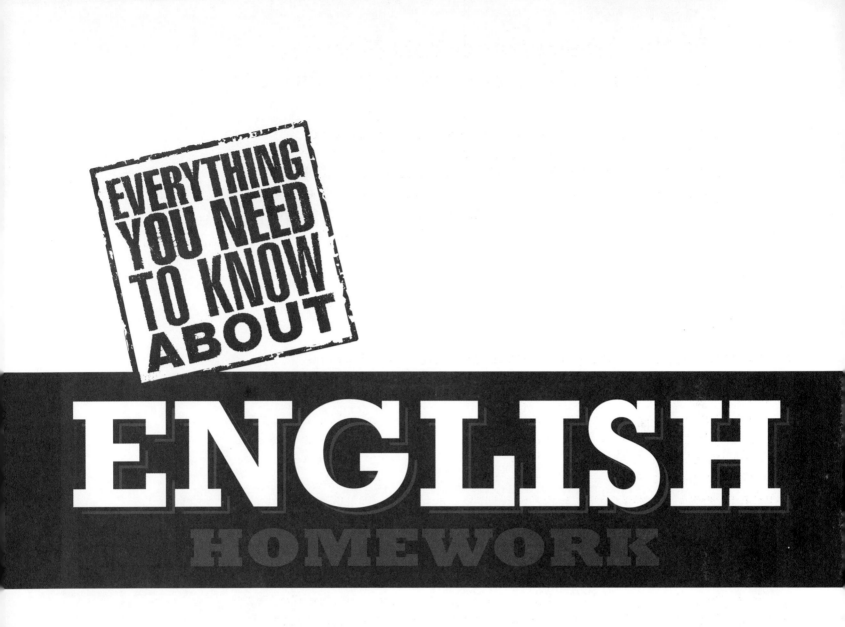

EVERYTHING YOU NEED TO KNOW ABOUT

# ENGLISH
## HOMEWORK

# Languages and Alphabets

## Chapter 1 Languages

### LANGUAGES SPOKEN AROUND THE WORLD

About 4,000 languages are spoken throughout the world today. Many of them are spoken by only a few people and within a small area.

Some people speak more than one language. In the United States, for example, many families come from other countries. Although these families learn English when they settle here, they may still speak the language of their home country. In some countries, people speak one language at home and another for business and politics. All people who can speak two languages are **bilingual**.

Today, English is often spoken in international business and politics. It is called an **international language**. For example, if a Japanese person wants to buy land from a person in Poland, unless they have an interpreter, the Japanese person and the Polish person will probably speak to each other in English. Spanish and French are two other international languages.

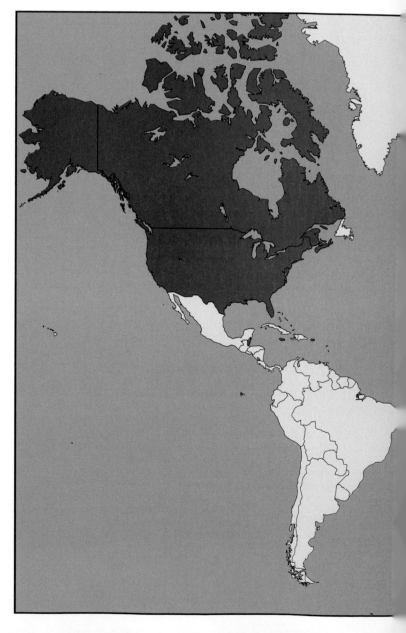

*Places around the world where English is spoken are in red.*

2

# The World's Most Commonly Spoken Languages

| Language | Number of Speakers |
|----------|--------------------|
| Mandarin | more than 1,000,000,000 |
| English | 490,000,000 |
| Hindi | nearly 435,000,000 |
| Spanish | nearly 400,000,000 |
| Russian | 285,000,000 |
| Arabic | 230,000,000 |

# Indo-European Languages

The languages of the world are grouped into *families*. These families include languages that are related to each other. Most *linguists* (see p. 5) believe that the languages in each family grew out of one ancient language.

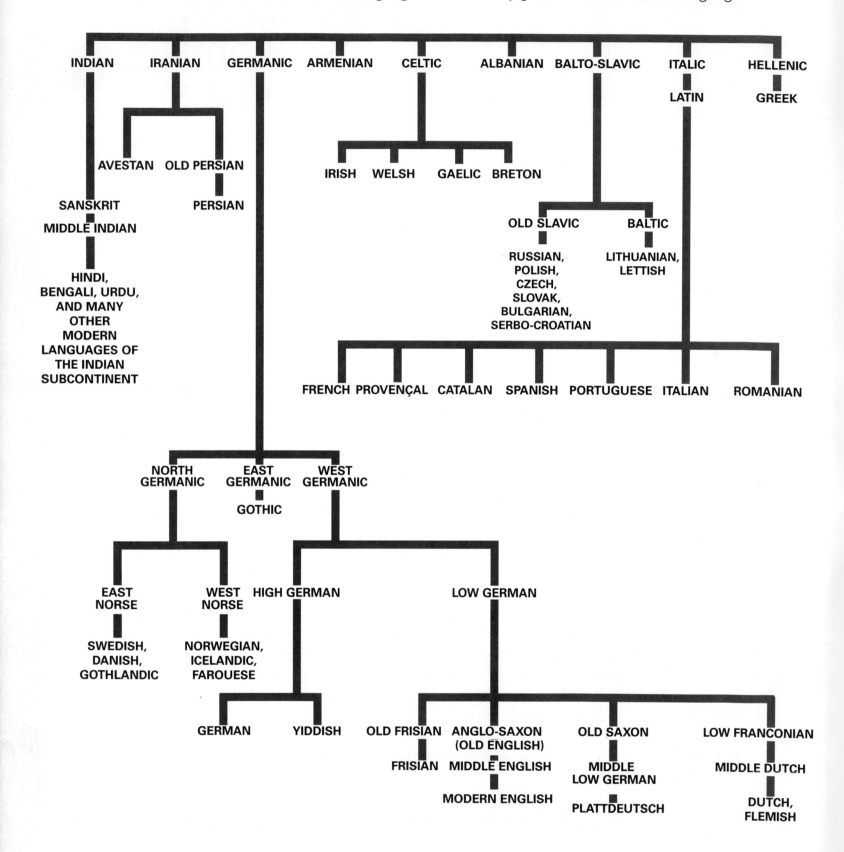

INDIAN    IRANIAN    GERMANIC    ARMENIAN    CELTIC    ALBANIAN    BALTO-SLAVIC    ITALIC    HELLENIC

AVESTAN    OLD PERSIAN

LATIN

GREEK

SANSKRIT

PERSIAN

IRISH    WELSH    GAELIC    BRETON

MIDDLE INDIAN

OLD SLAVIC    BALTIC

HINDI,
BENGALI, URDU,
AND MANY
OTHER
MODERN
LANGUAGES OF
THE INDIAN
SUBCONTINENT

RUSSIAN,
POLISH,
CZECH,
SLOVAK,
BULGARIAN,
SERBO-CROATIAN

LITHUANIAN,
LETTISH

FRENCH    PROVENÇAL    CATALAN    SPANISH    PORTUGUESE    ITALIAN    ROMANIAN

NORTH
GERMANIC    EAST
GERMANIC    WEST
GERMANIC

GOTHIC

EAST
NORSE    WEST
NORSE    HIGH GERMAN    LOW GERMAN

SWEDISH,
DANISH,
GOTHLANDIC

NORWEGIAN,
ICELANDIC,
FAROUESE

GERMAN    YIDDISH    OLD FRISIAN    ANGLO-SAXON
(OLD ENGLISH)    OLD SAXON    LOW FRANCONIAN

FRISIAN    MIDDLE ENGLISH    MIDDLE
LOW GERMAN    MIDDLE DUTCH

MODERN ENGLISH    PLATTDEUTSCH    DUTCH,
FLEMISH

Here is the word **mother** in some Indo-European languages. Can you see how they are related?

| | |
|---|---|
| Dutch | **moeder** |
| French | **mère** |
| German | **mutter** |
| Hindi | **mata** |
| Italian | **madre** |
| Spanish | **madre** |

> Some words are related through ancestral descent, derivation, or borrowing. These words are called *cognates*.

# The Scientists of Language

The study of language is called *linguistics*. The people who study language are called linguists. The different types of linguists include the following:

*Grammarians*. People who study grammar. *Grammar* means the parts of a language and the rules for speaking and writing that language.

*Phoneticians* or *phonetists*. Those who study *phonetics*. Phonetics is the study of sounds in speech. Phoneticians study how the tongue, lips, and teeth are positioned in order to make different sounds. The study of speech sounds, *phonemics*, is part of phonetics. When you study *phonics* in school, you are studying an area of phonetics.

*Semanticians*. Linguists who study *semantics*. Semantics is the study of the meanings of sounds and words. *Morphemics*, the study of units of sound that carry meaning, is part of semantics.

*Morphologists*. People who study *morphology*. Morphology is the study of how language changes over time and in different places. For example, some morphologists are concerned with the difference between Old English (used about 450–1100), Middle English (used about 1100–1500), and Modern English (used today). Other morphologists are concerned with the different ways the same language is spoken in different places. For example, they might compare English in such countries as the United States, Canada, Great Britain, and Australia, or Spanish in Spain, Mexico, and Peru.

*Philologists*. Those who study *philology*. Philology is the study of how the language of a culture affects its literature.

# Chapter 2

# Alphabets

## A History of Our Alphabet

In English, we use a set of 26 letters to spell words:

**A B C D E F G H I J K L M N O P Q R S T U V W X Y Z**

This set of letters is our **alphabet**.

Our alphabet is called the Latin or Roman alphabet. Except for the letters **j**, **u**, and **w**, it was the alphabet used by the Romans 2,000 years ago. At first, the Roman alphabet had only 21 letters. Around 100 B.C., the letters **y** and **z** were added. **J**, **u**, and **w** were added much later to represent sounds spelled before with **y** and **v**, as well as to represent new sounds.

### WHERE DID THE ROMAN ALPHABET COME FROM?

The Romans used the Etruscan alphabet to design their own alphabet. The Etruscans were people who lived in northern Italy about 8,000 years ago. The Etruscan alphabet grew out of the ancient Greek alphabet. The ancient Greeks borrowed the alphabet of an even more ancient group of people, the Phoenicians. About 10,000 years ago, the Phoenicians lived in Byblos, a city in modern Lebanon. Byblos was a center for trading **papyrus**, a reed that was made into paperlike sheets of material. Our word **paper** comes from the word papyrus. The Greek word for book, **byblos**, comes from the name of the city Byblos. **Byblos** is also the root of our word **Bible**.

Phoenician

| Early Greek | Later Greek | Roman | English |
| --- | --- | --- | --- |
| | | A | A |
| | | B | B |
| | | CG | CG |
| | | D | D |
| | | E | E |
| | | FV | F,U,V,W,Y |
| | | | Z |
| | | H | H |
| | | | (Th) |
| | | I | I,J |
| | | | K |
| | | L | K |
| | | M | L |
| | | N | M |
| | | O | N |
| | | P | O |
| | | | P |
| | | | (S) |
| | | Q | Q |
| | | R | R |
| | | S | S |
| | | T | T |

7

# HIEROGLYPHICS, PICTOGRAPHS, AND SYLLABARIES

**Hieroglyphics** are sets of special picture symbols used to write down stories or information. Among the best-known hieroglyphics are those used by the ancient Egyptians, who created an elaborate set of picture symbols to describe daily life, farming, and the wealth of pharaohs. Egyptian hieroglyphics are easy to recognize but they are difficult to read. Reading hieroglyphics is so difficult, in fact, that the word **hieroglyphics** also means any handwriting, figures, codes, or characters that are hard to understand or decipher.

   **Pictographs** are picture signs and symbols that tell a story, although the signs and symbols aren't organized into a set. The pictures drawn on cave walls by early humans are pictographs telling stories of daily life, hunting, fishing, gathering, and so on. Pictographs are still used today to chart information by using picture symbols to represent special kinds of information.

   **Syllabaries** are sets of symbols. In a syllabary, each symbol represents a specific syllable that can be used in many different words. A syllabary was used instead of an alphabet in the writing systems of some ancient cultures and is still used today. The two sets of characters used in writing Japanese are modern examples of syllabaries.

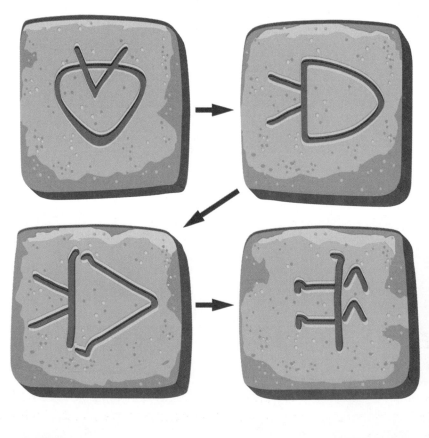

*The early cuneiform symbol for an ox evolved from pictographs.*

## CAPITAL AND SMALL LETTERS

Until about 200 years ago, only a small group of people could read and write. Some of these people, called **engravers**, cut (engraved) words and dates into stone tablets or into the faces of buildings or monuments. The engravers used capital letters, which they carved in simple lines and curves into the stone.

Later, people called **scribes** were trained to write on papyrus and parchment. Papyrus and parchment were very expensive, so scribes had to fit as many words as they could on each precious page. Scribes also had to copy huge books such as the Bible, so they needed to write quickly.

Although capital letters were easy to engrave in stone, they were too large and difficult to form quickly when written with quill pens. So scribes developed **cursive** letters that flowed more easily together. At first, they rounded capital letters into **uncials**. By 1000 A.D., they had created a version of the Roman alphabet in small letters. By combining cursive capital letters with small letters, scribes had a system of writing that saved space and time.

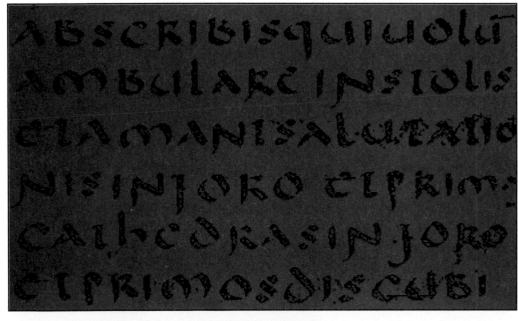

*An early scribe wrote uncials on this sample of a manuscript created with ink on parchment.*

## UPPERCASE AND LOWERCASE

Today we call capital letters **uppercase** letters. We call small letters **lowercase** letters. The terms **uppercase** and **lowercase** came about with the invention of printing presses.

# Alphabet Spin-offs

Many alphabets are used in the world today. Some are closely related to the Roman alphabet. For example, the *Celtic alphabet* is still used in Ireland and Scotland to write the Gaelic language. The *Cyrillic alphabet*—used in Serbia, Bulgaria, the Ukraine, and Russia—was adapted from the Greek alphabet. The *Chinese* created an alphabet based on pictures called *characters*. The *Japanese* and *Korean alphabets* are based on characters, too.

## READING FROM RIGHT TO LEFT AND TOP TO BOTTOM

*Roman*, *Greek*, and related alphabets are read from left to right. So is the *Hindi* alphabet, which is used in parts of India and Africa. But some alphabets, such as *Arabic* and *Hebrew*, are read from right to left. Still other alphabets, like the *Chinese*, are read from top to bottom.

הפך בה והפך
בה דכולא בה
כתבו לכם את
השירה הזאת

*Hebrew is read from right to left.*

兒童百科全書

*Chinese is read from top to bottom.*

10

# Chapter 3 Sign and Symbol Languages

## Sign Language

When people have difficulty hearing or cannot hear at all, spoken language is often not effective. **Sign language** was developed as another way for the hearing impaired to communicate. Signs that stand for letters and whole words are made by shaping fingers and hands in different ways. People can have a conversation using sign language.

 A  B  C  D E  F

G H I J K

 L  M  N  O  P

 Q R S T U

V W X  Y  Z

11

# Braille

Reading words on a page can be difficult for people with poor eyesight and impossible for people who are blind. In the late 1820s, **Louis Braille**, himself a blind man, invented a special alphabet for people with sight problems. The **Braille alphabet** consists of raised dots that are read by touch, not sight. Each letter has its own set of dots. The letters are written on paper held by a frame. The writer uses a pointed stick, or **stylus**, to make the dots. Today many blind people use machines similar to typewriters to make the dots.

| A | B | C | D | E | F | G | H | I | J |
|---|---|---|---|---|---|---|---|---|---|

| K | L | M | N | O | P | Q | R | S | T |
|---|---|---|---|---|---|---|---|---|---|

| U | V | W | X | Y | Z | and | for | of | the |
|---|---|---|---|---|---|---|---|---|---|

| with | ch | gh | sh | th | wh | ed | er | ou | ow |
|---|---|---|---|---|---|---|---|---|---|

# Native American Sign Language and Smoke Signals

Ancient Native American cultures, including the Maya and Aztecs of Mexico and Central America, created writing systems made up of **glyphs**, or pictures. In North America, Sequoya, a Cherokee, invented a writing system made up of 86 signs that stood for the different sounds in the Cherokee language. Each tribe spoke a different language, so Native Americans from different tribes invented a simple sign language to facilitate communication.

Native Americans on the Great Plains also communicated by smoke signals. The signals could be seen over many miles. By using smoke signals for basic communication, messengers were not needed to travel long distances over dangerous routes.

*arrow*

*trade*

*friend*

*buffalo*

*horse*

*tepee*

*Native American*

*caucasian*

*peace*

# Semaphore

Sailors can't shout loudly enough over the noise of wind and waves to be heard on passing ships, and hand signs are impossible to read over the distances at sea. So sailors use **semaphore**. In semaphore, sailors use brightly colored flags in different patterns and angles to represent different letters and messages. The flags can be seen easily across the water.

# Morse Code

The telegraph was patented in 1837 by American artist **Samuel F. B. Morse**. In its day, the telegraph was the only machine that could send instant messages across long distances. It worked by sending messages in code through electric wires. The code, known as **Morse code**, consists of combinations of dots and dashes, which stand for the letters in the alphabet.

# Letter Sounds and Words

**Chapter 1**

# Vowel and Consonant Sounds

## Where Sounds Are Made

bilabial shape
(m,p,b,w)

alveolar shape
(t,d,ch,j,n)

linguadental shape
(s,z,sh)

labiodental shape
(f,v)

palatal shape
(y)

velar shape
(g,k)

# Vowels and Consonants

The English alphabet is made up of 26 letters. These letters are divided into two groups: **vowels** and **consonants**. There are 21 consonants

b c d f g h j k l m n p q r s t v w x y z

and five vowels

**a e i o u.**

The letter **y** sometimes serves as a vowel, for example, in the words **my, by, only,** and **symbol.**

# Picture Keys to Vowel Sounds

| Vowel | short | | long |
|---|---|---|---|

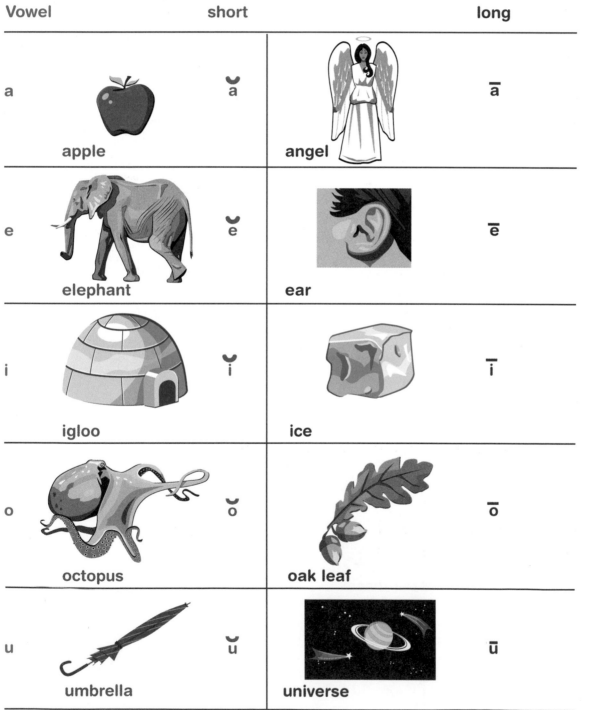

| | | short | | long |
|---|---|---|---|---|
| a | apple | ă | angel | ā |
| e | elephant | ĕ | ear | ē |
| i | igloo | ĭ | ice | ī |
| o | octopus | ŏ | oak leaf | ō |
| u | umbrella | ŭ | universe | ū |

16

# Vowel Digraphs

*Vowel digraphs* are usually two vowels written together. Some stand for the sound of a long vowel (ai, ea, ie, oa). Others stand for special vowel sounds (oi, ou, oo, au, ew).

| | | | |
|---|---|---|---|
| ai, ay | **pain, say** | ou, ow | **out, cow** |
| ea, ee | **bean, see** | oo | **boot, book (this digraph stands for two different sounds)** |
| ie, igh | **tie, high** | | |
| oa, oe, ow | **boat, toe, snow** | au, aw | **sauce, claw** |
| oi, oy | **boil, toy** | ew, ue | **grew, blue** |

Other common vowel spelling patterns:

| | |
|---|---|
| ight | **height, night** |
| all | **ball** |
| alk, alt | **walk, salt** |
| ild, ind | **wild, find** |
| old | **told** |
| ear, eer | **fear, deer** |

# Blends

*Blends* are two or more consonants that keep their regular sounds when combined. Blends may appear at the beginning, middle, or end of words.

Some common beginning blends are bl, br, cl, cr, dr, fl, fr, gl, gr, pl, pr, sk, sl, sm, sn, st, and tr.

Some common ending blends are ft, mp, nd, and nt.

Sometimes when two or more consonants are written together, they stand for a new sound. These blends are called *digraphs*.

| | |
|---|---|
| ch, tch | **chair, match** |
| sh | **ship, wish** |
| th | **thin, that (stands for two sounds—voiced and unvoiced)** |
| wh | **whale** |
| ph | **phone** |

Sometimes when two or more consonants are written together, one of the letters is silent.

| | |
|---|---|
| kn | **know** |
| wr | **write** |
| gn | **gnat** |
| mb | **comb** |

# Voiced and Unvoiced

Sounds can be *voiced* or *unvoiced*. A voiced sound is made by vibrating the vocal cords with air from the lungs. All vowels are voiced. Unvoiced sounds are made without vibrating the vocal cords, and often using the tongue and teeth. Many consonants are unvoiced.

# Schwa

The *schwa* is the vowel sound heard in an unstressed syllable ('). The symbol for schwa looks like an upside-down small *e*. Schwa sounds like a short *u* (u or uh). For example:

**syllable = sil ə bə l**

(See also Pronunciation Keys, p. 37.)

# Accentuate the Syllable

Syllables are words or parts of words in which a vowel sound is heard. Syllables can be simple phonemes, or sounds that have no particular meaning. Syllables can also be morphemes, or sounds that have meaning. Accents tell which syllable in a word receives emphasis.
For example:

**banana = ba nan´a**          **friendship = friend´ ship**

Sometimes more than one syllable is stressed. The louder syllable takes the *primary accent*. The less loud stressed syllable takes the *secondary accent*. For example:

**elementary = el´ e men´ ta ry**          **cafeteria = caf´ e te´ ri a**

# Chapter 2 Prefixes, Suffixes, and Roots

## Prefixes

**Prefixes** are groups of letters that have meaning and are at the beginnings of words. When a prefix is attached to a word, its meaning combines with the meaning of the original word to form a new word. **Prefix** is a good example. **Pre-** comes from Latin and means "before." **Fix** means "to attach." So **prefix** means "to attach before"—in this case, to attach before a word.

### COMMON GREEK AND LATIN PREFIXES

| Prefix | Origin | Meaning | Example |
|--------|--------|---------|---------|
| acro- | Greek | top, high | acrobat (walker up high) |
| aero- | Greek | air | aerobic (using air) |
| alti- | Latin | high | altitude (height) |
| amphi- | Greek | both, around | amphibian (living in both air and water) |
| ana- | Greek | not, wrong | anachronism (in the wrong time frame) |
| andro- | Greek | man | android (robot with human features) |
| ante- | Latin | before | antebellum (before the war, usually the Civil War) |
| anthro- | Greek | man | anthropology (study of humans) |
| aqua-, aque- | Latin | water | aquarium (water-filled tank) |
| arch(i)- | Greek | chief, main | architect (building designer) |
| archaeo- | Greek | very old | archaeology (study of human life in the past) |
| arthro- | Greek | joint | arthropod (animals, usually insects, with jointed legs) |
| astro- | Greek | star | asteroid (star that moves through space) |
| atmo- | Greek | vapor, gas | atmosphere (layer of gases surrounding a planet) |
| audio- | Latin | sound, hearing | audiometer (instrument used to test hearing) |
| baro- | Greek | weight | barometer (instrument that measures air pressure) |
| biblio- | Greek | book | bibliography (list of books) |
| bio- | Greek | life, living | biology (the science of living things) |
| centi- | Latin | hundred | centipede (100-legged arthropod) |
| chloro- | Greek | green | chlorophyll (substance that makes plants green) |

*prefix*    **+**    *word*    **=**    *new word*

| Prefix | Origin | Meaning | Example |
| --- | --- | --- | --- |
| chrono- | Greek | time | chronology (list of events in the order in which they happened) |
| circum- | Latin | around | circumference (distance around a circle or sphere) |
| co- | Latin | together | cooperate (work together) |
| contra- | Latin | against | contradict (say the opposite) |
| cosmo- | Greek | universe | cosmic (having to do with the universe) |
| crypto- | Greek | hidden, secret | cryptogram (message written in code) |
| de- | Latin | not, put down | deny (say something is not true) |
| deca- | Greek | ten | decade (10 years) |
| deci- | Latin | tenth | decimal (based on the number 10) |
| denti- | Latin | tooth | dentist (tooth doctor) |
| di(s)- | Latin | apart | disconnect (take apart) |
| dia- | Greek | through | diameter (straight line that passes through the center of a circle) |
| digit- | Latin | finger | digits (the numbers 0 through 9; fingers and toes) |
| dino- | Greek | terrible | dinosaur (terrible lizard) |
| dyna- | Greek | force | dynamite (powerful explosive) |
| equi- | Latin | equal | equivalent (equal in amount, value, or meaning) |
| geo- | Greek | earth, land | geography (study of Earth's surface) |
| glosso- | Greek | tongue | glossary (list of words and their meanings) |
| grapho- | Greek | written, writing | graphology (study of handwriting) |
| helio- | Greek | sun | heliocentric (arrangement of planets with a sun in the center, as in our solar system) |
| hemi- | Greek | half | hemisphere (half of a sphere) |
| hetero- | Greek | different | heterogeneous (made up of different parts) |
| hexa- | Greek | six | hexagon (flat figure with six sides and six angles) |
| homo- | Greek | same | homophones (words that sound the same) |
| hydro- | Greek | water | hydroelectric (electricity coming from waterpower) |
| hypno- | Greek | sleep | hypnotize (to relax someone into a sleeplike condition) |
| il-, im- | Latin | not, against | illegal, imperfect (against the law; not perfect) |
| inter- | Latin | between | interplanetary (between planets) |
| intra-, intro- | Latin | inside | introduce (make known; bring inside) |
| iso- | Greek | equal | isosceles triangle (triangle with two equal sides) |
| magni- | Latin | great | magnificent (great in beauty, importance, or decoration) |
| mal(e)- | Latin | evil, bad | malice (bad feeling, wanting to do evil things to others) |
| mega- | Greek | great | megaphone (cone-shaped tube that, when talked through, makes the human voice louder or greater) |
| metro- | Greek | measure | meter (basic unit of measuring length in the metric system) |

| Prefix | Origin | Meaning | Example |
|---|---|---|---|
| micro- | Greek | small | microscope (instrument that makes small things appear larger) |
| mono- | Greek | one | monotone (unchanging tone or pitch; drone) |
| multi- | Latin | many | multitude (many people or things) |
| neo- | Greek | new | neonatal (newborn) |
| nocti- | Latin | night | nocturnal (active at night) |
| ob- | Latin | against | object (go against) |
| octa- | Latin | eight | octagon (flat figure with eight sides and eight angles) |
| omni- | Latin | all | omnivore (animal that eats both plants and animals) |
| ped- , pedi- | Latin | foot | pedal (foot-operated lever) |
| pedo- , pedi- | Greek | child | pediatrician (doctor for babies and children) |
| per- | Latin | thorough, complete | perfect (complete in every way) |
| poly- | Greek | many | polygon (flat figure with many sides) |
| post- | Latin | after | postscript, P.S. (note added after the signature on a letter) |
| pre- | Latin | before | previous (event that happened before) |
| pro- | Latin | for | promote (work for the growth or success of a person, idea, company, etc.) |
| re- | Latin | again | return (come again) |
| retro- | Latin | backward | retrorocket (rocket fired in the opposite direction of a larger rocket to slow it down) |
| rhino- | Greek | nose | rhinoceros (large mammal with one or two large horns on its snout) |
| sub- | Latin | below, under | submerge (put under water) |
| super-, supra- | Latin | above | superior (in a position above) |
| terra- | Latin | land | terrarium (glass tank used to grow plants or raise small land animals) |
| trans- | Latin | over, across, beyond | transport (carry over land, water, or through air) |
| ultra- | Latin | beyond | ultrasonic (having to do with sounds that are beyond the ability of humans to hear) |
| uni- | Latin | one | unicorn (imaginary horselike animal with one horn growing from the top of its head) |

# Suffixes

**Suffixes**, like prefixes, combine their meanings with the meaning of the words to which they are added to form new words. But suffixes are "fixed," or attached, to the **ends** of words.

Many suffixes change the original word from one **part of speech** to another. For example, the suffix **-er** changes the verb **teach** to the noun **teacher**. The suffix **-er** also is used to make comparisons. My dog is **nice** but my cat is **nicer**. The suffix **-ing** is also used to change one part of speech to another, often a verb to a noun. For example, **teach** to **teaching** (see also Gerunds, p. 55). The suffix **-ing** is also used to form present participles (see p. 45). Another common suffix in English is **-ed**. It is used to form the past participles of regular verbs (see p. 45) and to form adjectives from nouns. For example, *Robin Milligan has a strong will. The strong-willed student is Robin Milligan.*

# Adding Suffixes

Adding suffixes can be as simple as adding a suffix to a root word, with no changes in spelling of either the root word or the suffix. But there are some cases when the spelling of root words changes in order to receive a suffix. Following are some rules for adding suffixes to different types of root words.

Unless a root word ends in **y**, simply add **-ly**.

| | | |
|---|---|---|
| mere + ly | = | merely |
| kind + ly | = | kindly |
| bold + ly | = | boldly |

Exceptions to this rule include:

| | | |
|---|---|---|
| true + ly | = | truly |
| whole + ly | = | wholly |
| simple + ly | = | simply |

For root words that end in **y**, change the **y** to **i** and add suffixes that begin with consonants, such as **-ly**, **-ness**, **-ful**, and **-ment**.

| | | |
|---|---|---|
| wary + ly | = | warily |
| naughty + ness | = | naughtiness |
| beauty + ful | = | beautiful |
| merry + ment | = | merriment |

If a suffix begins with a consonant, it can usually be added to a root word that ends in a consonant or in a silent **e**.

| | | |
|---|---|---|
| kind + ness | = | kindness |
| nice + ness | = | niceness |
| govern + ment | = | government |
| induce + ment | = | inducement |
| certain + ly | = | certainly |
| sincere + ly | = | sincerely |
| art + ful | = | artful |
| shame + ful | = | shameful |

Exceptions to this rule include:

**judgment  truly  wholly**

If a suffix begins with a vowel — **-ed**, **-ing**, **-ate**, **-ous**, **-ably**, **-al**, or **-y** — drop the silent **e** at the end of a root word.

| | | |
|---|---|---|
| hope + ed | = | hoped |
| race + ing | = | racing |
| fame + ous | = | famous |
| nature + al | = | natural |
| laze + y | = | lazy |
| fortune + ate | = | fortunate |

Double the final consonant of a one-syllable root word that ends in a vowel followed by a consonant before adding a suffix that begins with a vowel.

| | | |
|---|---|---|
| bat + t + ing | = | batting |
| flip + p + ed | = | flipped |
| hot + t + er | = | hotter |

In root words that end in **y**, change the **y** to **i** before adding the suffixes **-age**, **-ly**, or **-ness**.

| | | |
|---|---|---|
| carry + age | = | carriage |
| busy + ly | = | busily |
| happy + ness | = | happiness |

# COMMON GREEK AND LATIN SUFFIXES

| SUFFIX | ORIGIN | MEANING | EXAMPLE |
|---|---|---|---|
| -archy | Greek | rule | monarchy (state or country ruled by a king, a queen, or an emperor) |
| -biosis | Greek | life | symbiosis (two or more living things that support each other) |
| -chrome | Greek | color | monochrome (picture presented in one color only) |
| -cide | Latin | kill | homicide (murder) |
| -cracy | Greek | form of rule | democracy (government run by people, not by a king, a queen, an emperor, or a dictator) |
| -derm | Greek | skin | epidermis (outer layer of skin) |
| -drome | Greek | running | hippodrome (arena for horse race or show) |
| -emia | Greek | of the blood | anemia (blood without enough red blood cells) |
| -fuge | Latin | away from | refuge (shelter or protection from danger) |
| -gamy | Greek | marriage | monogamy (marriage to one person at a time) |
| -geny | Greek | bearing | progeny (children) |
| -gon | Greek | angle | polygon (flat figure with four or more angles) |
| -grade | Latin | walking | centigrade (scale for measuring progressing temperature, from freezing at 0° to boiling at 100°) |
| -gram, -graph | Greek | writing | telegraph (message sent by a device that uses electrical wires) |
| -hedron | Greek | having sides | polyhedron (solid figure with many sides) |
| -iatrics | Greek | treatment of disease | geriatrics (medical treatment of senior citizens) |
| -itis | Greek | disease | arthritis (joint disease) |
| -lepsy | Greek | attack | narcolepsy (sudden attack of sleepiness) |
| -lith | Greek | made of stone | monolith (large freestanding stone) |
| -logy | Greek | spoken, a theory, or science | paleontology (science of prehistoric life) |
| -mania | Greek | type of madness | kleptomania (uncontrollable desire to steal) |
| -meter | Greek | instrument | thermometer (instrument used for measuring temperature) |
| -nomy | Greek | laws ruling | astronomy (science of outer space) |
| -oid | Greek | in the form of | asteroid (small bodies in space that orbit the sun) |
| -opia | Greek | of the eye | myopia (nearsightedness) |
| -ous | Latin | having the qualities of, full | beauteous (having the qualities of beauty) |
| -pathy | Greek | feeling, suffering | antipathy (strong feeling of dislike) |
| -phany | Greek | appearance | epiphany (sudden appearance of the solution to a problem, or the meaning of a phrase or sentence, etc.) |
| -phobia | Greek | fear, dread | claustrophobia (fear of being closed into small places) |
| -phone | Greek | sound | homophone (sound that is the same as another but spelled differently) |

# COMMON GREEK AND LATIN ROOTS

The **root** is the main part of a word, the part that contains the basic meaning.

| ROOT | ORIGIN | MEANING | EXAMPLE |
|---|---|---|---|
| act | Latin | do | action, activity |
| anim | Latin | breath/spirit | animation, animal |
| art | Latin | skill | artistic, artisan |
| cardi | Latin | heart | cardiac, cardiologist |
| clar | Latin | clear | clarity, declare, clarification |
| cogn | Latin | know | recognize, cognition, incognito |
| cred | Latin | believe | incredible, credibility |
| cycle | Greek | wheel/circle | bicycle, cyclone |
| dent | Latin | tooth | dentist, dentures |
| duc/duct | Latin | convey/lead | conduct, educate |
| fac | Latin | make/do | factory, factor |
| fract/frag | Latin | break | fragment, fracture |
| gen | Latin | birth | generation, congenital |
| gram | Greek | write/letter | grammar, diagram |
| grat | Latin | pleasing | gratitude, grateful |
| imag | Latin | imitate/likeness | image, imagination |
| lab | Latin | work | labor, elaborate, laboratory |
| loc | Latin | place | location, dislocate |
| luna | Latin | moon | lunar, lunatic |
| man | Latin | hand | manual, manuscript |
| mand | Latin | to order | mandatory, command |
| max | Latin | most | maximum |
| merge | Latin | dip/dive | submerge, emerge |
| meter | Greek | measure | millimeter, thermometer |
| mob | Latin | move | mobile, automobile |
| mort | Latin | death | mortal, mortify |
| mov | Latin | move | movie, remove |

| ROOT | ORIGIN | MEANING | EXAMPLE |
|------|--------|---------|---------|
| narr | Latin | tell | narrate |
| nav | Latin | ship | navigator, naval |
| neg | Latin | no | negative, negate |
| nov | Latin | new | innovation, novel |
| opt | Latin | best | optimal, optimize |
| pater | Latin | father | paternal, patriarch |
| port | Latin | carry | portable, import, deport |
| psych | Greek | mind/soul | psychiatry, psychic |
| put | Latin | thing | compute, putative, dispute |
| san | Latin | health | sanitary, sane |
| sci | Latin | know | conscious, science |
| sol | Latin | alone | solo, solitary |
| spec | Latin | see/look | spectator, speculate |
| sphere | Latin | ball | hemisphere, atmosphere |
| sum | Latin | highest | summate, summary |
| temp | Latin | time | tempo, comtemporary |
| term | Latin | end | terminal, determine |
| terr | Latin | land/earth | terrain, territory |
| therm | Greek | heat | thermal, thermometer |
| tox | Greek | poison | toxic, toxin |
| urb | Latin | city | urban, urbane, suburb |
| vac | Latin | empty | vacuum, vacant, evacuate |
| vid/vis | Latin | see | video, vision |
| voc | Greek | voice | vocation, invoke |

# Chapter 3

# Spelling Sounds and Words

## Five Basic Rules for Spelling

**1 Words containing ie or ei**

*I* before *e*, except after *c*, or when sounding like *a*, as in **neighbor** and **weigh**.

| I before E | | Except after C | Sounding as A |
|---|---|---|---|
| die | grief | ceiling | sleigh |
| lie | chief | receipt | vein |
| tie | believe | deceive | eight |

> **Exceptions to the "i before e" rule include** ceiling, conceit, either, foreign, height, leisure, neither, sheik, species, **and** weird.

**2 Silent or final e**

If a word ends with a silent *e*, drop the *e* before adding a suffix that begins with a vowel.

*bore/boring     love/loving     skate/skating*

Do not drop the silent *e* before adding a suffix that begins with a consonant.

*bore/boredom     hate/hateful     skate/skateboard*

> **Exceptions to the "silent e" rule include** argument, ninth, **and** truly.

**3 Final y**

If a word ends in a consonant followed by *y*, change the *y* to *i* before adding a suffix.

*cry/cried     friendly/friendliness     gloomy/gloominess*

If a word ends in *y* with a vowel before it, do not change *y* to *i* before adding suffixes or other endings.

*destroy/destroyed     play/playing     volley/volleys*

> **If a suffix begins with i, do not change the y, for example:** crying, dryish.

**4 Consonant preceded by a vowel**

If a one-syllable word ends with one consonant with a vowel before it, double the final consonant before adding a suffix.

*can/canned     nut/nutty     pot/pottery*

If a multisyllable word ends with a consonant preceded by a vowel and the accent is on the last syllable, double the final consonant before adding a suffix.

*acquit/acquittal     control/controlling     repel/repellent*

**5 One-plus-one rule**

When a prefix ends in the same letter with which the main word begins, include both of the repeated letters.

*il- + logical = illogical     mis- + spell = misspell*

When a suffix begins with the same letter with which a main word ends, include both the repeated letters.

*accidental + ly = accidentally     mean + ness = meanness*

The one-plus-one rule also applies to making compound words. Include all letters of both words, even if they are repeated.

*room + mate = roommate*

> **If a word with more than one syllable ends in a consonant preceded by a vowel but the last syllable is unaccented, do not double the consonant before adding a suffix, for example:** travel/traveler, honor/honorable, **and** widen/widened.

# Commonly Mispelled Words
*(s inserted to make "Misspelled")*

| | | | |
|---|---|---|---|
| accessory | conscience | government | omitted |
| accompany | conscious | grammar | parallel |
| acquaintance | corduroy | guarantee | plaid |
| acquire | cough | guess | potatoes |
| address | counterfeit | guest | prairie |
| all right | debt | handkerchief | privilege |
| a lot | definite | height | probably |
| already | dependent | independence | raspberry |
| Antarctic | desperate | judgment | receipt |
| arithmetic | diarrhea | kindergarten | reference |
| asthma | disappear | laugh | relieve |
| athlete | dumb | league | rhythm |
| available | eighth | library | ridiculous |
| banana | environment | license | sandwich |
| bargain | exaggerate | literature | scissors |
| beauty | exceed | maintenance | separately |
| believe | excel | mathematics | special |
| broccoli | exercise | mattress | squirrel |
| calendar | exist | misspell | tomatoes |
| cantaloupe | fascinate | mosquitoes | truly |
| caterpillar | February | necessary | Tuesday |
| ceiling | forehead | neighbor | usually |
| cemetery | formally | niece | vaccinate |
| chief | formerly | noticeable | vacuum |
| cinnamon | freight | nuisance | Wednesday |
| committee | gauge | obedience | |
| congratulations | glacier | occurred | |

# Homophones, Homonyms, and Homographs

**Homophones** are sounds that are the same but are spelled differently. For example, **f** and **ph** are often used to spell the same sound, as in:

### fine or file and phone or physical

**C** and **s** can also spell the same sound, as in:

### circus or cereal and symbol or sign

And **g** and **j** can also spell the same sound, as in:

### refuge or sergeant and jump or jinx

The word **homophone** comes from the Greek words **homo** (same) and **phone** (sound). It is also used to describe **homonyms**, or words that sound the same but have different meanings. The word **homonym** also comes from Greek words **homo** and **onyma** (name). (See also The Secret of Nyms, p. 36.)

> Homonyms that not only sound the same but are also spelled the same are called *homographs*. The word *homograph* comes from the Greek words *homo* and *graph*, which mean "same writing" (see Prefixes, Suffixes, and Roots, pp. 19–25).

Please mail this letter.
The letter came in the mail.
The knight wore armor and chain mail.

We wore our swimsuits to the pool.
Mom drives to work in a car pool.
I have a pool table in my basement.

## Familiar Homonyms

| | |
|---|---|
| allowed/aloud | I was **allowed** to play my stereo after school.<br>We read **aloud** in class. |
| ant/aunt | The **ant** is a frequent visitor at picnics.<br>My **aunt** is my father's sister. |
| ate/eight | I **ate** lunch at school last week.<br>I have **eight** video games. |
| bare/bear | Don't walk outside in your **bare** feet.<br>The **bear** lives in the woods. |
| berry/bury | The **berry** from that bush is poisonous.<br>The squirrel tried to **bury** the acorn. |
| blew/blue | The storm **blew** in from the west.<br>**Blue** is my favorite color. |
| brake/break | I had to **brake** to slow down my bicycle.<br>I didn't mean to **break** the glass vase. |
| capital/capitol | Please remember where to use **capital** letters.<br>We met Senator Smith in the **capitol** building. |
| cent/scent/sent | I don't have a **cent** to my name!<br>That perfume has an awful **scent**.<br>I **sent** a letter to my best friend. |
| colonel/kernel | The **colonel** led the soldiers in battle.<br>I found only one unpopped **kernel** in the popcorn bowl. |
| dear/deer | My puppy is very **dear** to me.<br>I saw some **deer** at the petting zoo. |
| fair/fare | The weather is **fair** today.<br>I paid full **fare** for my airplane ticket. |
| feat/feet | The acrobat performed a breathtaking **feat** on the high wire.<br>My **feet** hurt from standing too long. |
| flew/flu/flue | The birds **flew** past my window.<br>I had the **flu** over spring vacation.<br>The smoke and ash rose up the chimney **flue**. |
| flour/flower | We'll need some **flour** to make the pancake batter.<br>The violet is our state **flower**. |
| heal/heel/he'll | That scratch should **heal** quickly.<br>My new shoes rubbed a blister on my **heel**.<br>**He'll** be coming 'round the mountain when he comes. |

| | |
|---|---|
| hear/here | Please speak louder because I can't **hear** you.<br>Come over **here**! |
| heard/herd | I **heard** the news on the radio.<br>A **herd** of cattle moves to the lower pasture every afternoon. |
| hole/whole | My dog dug a **hole** in the backyard.<br>I read the **whole** book in one morning. |
| hour/our | I'll be ready in one **hour**.<br>**Our** next meeting is in one month. |
| know/no | I didn't **know** half the answers on the quiz.<br>**No**, I don't think I passed. |
| loan/lone | She asked him to **loan** her money for lunch.<br>When the other frogs left, Ribbet was the **lone** frog in the pond. |
| mail/male | I put the letter in the **mail** yesterday.<br>It was an all-**male** club and no girls could join. |
| main/mane | I think I understand the **main** idea of the story.<br>That male lion has a thick, beautiful **mane**. |
| meat/meet | I'm vegetarian now, so I don't eat **meat**.<br>**Meet** me at the mall at seven o'clock. |
| one/won | Give me **one** good reason for going to study hall.<br>Our team **won** at the science fair. |
| pail/pale | I took my little sister's **pail** and shovel to the beach.<br>Your face went **pale** when your name was called. |
| pain/pane | Cleaning my room is a real **pain**.<br>The window was made of one large **pane** of glass. |
| pair/pear | I have one **pair** of jeans.<br>The apple looks tastier than the **pear**. |
| peace/piece | The two countries signed a **peace** treaty.<br>I had a **piece** of that delicious chocolate cake. |
| plain/plane | The skirt was **plain**, but the blouse was fancy.<br>We flew on a **plane** to visit my grandfather. |
| pray/prey | Let's **pray** for good weather for our field trip.<br>Eagles and owls are birds of **prey**. |
| principal/principle | The **principal** idea of the story is that people should get along.<br>My teacher is a person of **principle**. |
| rain/reign/rein | The **rain** fell for two days before the sun came out again.<br>The queen's **reign** won't end until she dies.<br>She told me to take the horse by the **reins**. |
| right/write | Turn **right** at the corner.<br>**Write** a letter to your uncle. |
| role/roll | I auditioned for a **role** in the school play.<br>My favorite lunch is peanut butter and jelly on a **roll**. |
| sail/sale | The captain and crew set **sail** in their three-masted ship.<br>My mother says I can't get the jacket until it's on **sale**. |

| | |
|---|---|
| scene/seen | She painted a forest **scene** in art class. |
| | I haven't **seen** her since three o'clock. |
| soar/sore | Did you see the eagle **soar** through the sky? |
| | Throwing the ball made the new pitcher's arm **sore**. |
| some/sum | Have **some** pie if you're hungry. |
| | The **sum** of two and two is four. |
| son/sun | The father had one **son** and three daughters. |
| | The **sun** rises in the east. |
| stair/stare | It took the baby a long time to climb each **stair**. |
| | Looking around is fine, but please don't **stare**. |
| stationary/stationery | The statue is **stationary** so you can't move it. |
| | Use nice **stationery** for writing thank-you notes. |
| steal/steel | He used to **steal** pennies from his sister's piggy bank. |
| | The car body is made of **steel**. |
| suite/sweet | The **suite** of rooms was decorated in blue and green. |
| | The lemonade was too **sweet**. |
| tail/tale | My dog has a very long **tail**. |
| | Did you read the **tale** of Paul Bunyan and Babe, the blue ox? |
| their/there/they're | **Their** house is on the next block. |
| | Her dog is **there**, behind the fence. |
| | **They're** going to be happy after the quiz. |
| threw/through | She **threw** the ball past home plate. |
| | The ball flew **through** the air. |
| to/too/two | I went **to** the dance. |
| | My friend came, **too**. |
| | The **two** of us danced together. |
| waist/waste | I like my belt around my hips, not my **waist**. |
| | Don't **waste** that perfectly good paper. |
| wait/weight | Please **wait** for me. |
| | I'd guess your **weight** to be about 70 pounds. |
| way/weigh | Let's take the back **way** home. |
| | How many pounds do you **weigh**? |
| weak/week | She grew thin and **weak** from her illness. |
| | It took one **week** to recover. |
| wear/where | I thought I'd **wear** cutoffs to camp. |
| | **Where** did I put my homework? |
| weather/whether | The **weather** was warm and sunny. |
| | I don't know **whether** I should go or not. |
| which/witch | **Which** witch is **which**? |
| | The **witch** knew hundreds of spells. |

# PALINDROMES SEMORDNILAP

**mom**

**dad**

**noon**

**level**

**radar**

**Palindromes** are words, phrases, and sentences that read the same way forward and backward!

Madam, I'm Adam.

Able was I ere I saw Elba.

A man. A plan. A canal: Panama.

Rats live on no evil star.

# Abbreviations

**Abbreviations** are shortened forms of words. They are made by leaving letters out or by replacing a group of letters with another letter or symbol.

| | | | | |
|---|---|---|---|---|
| **AC** | alternating current (type of electrical current) | | **CIA** | Central Intelligence Agency |
| **A.D.** | anno Domini (Latin for "in the year of the Lord," or since the birth of Christ) | | **cm** | centimeter |
| | | | **COD** | cash on delivery |
| **a.m.** | ante meridiem (from midnight until noon) | | **CPA** | certified public accountant |
| | | | **CPR** | cardiopulmonary resuscitation |
| **asap** | as soon as possible | | **DA** | district attorney |
| **A.S.P.C.A.** | American Society for the Prevention of Cruelty to Animals | | **DC** | direct current (type of electrical current) |
| **BA** | Bachelor of Arts (college degree) | | **D.C.** | District of Columbia |
| **B.C.** | before Christ | | **DDS** | doctor of dental surgery |
| **B.C.E.** | before the Christian era | | **DNA** | deoxyribonucleic acid (the basic material of genes) |
| **BS** | Bachelor of Science | | | |
| **C** | centigrade or Celsius | | **DOA** | dead on arrival |
| **c.** | copyright or circa | | **ed.** | editor, edition |
| | | | **ESP** | extrasensory perception |

31

| | |
|---|---|
| **esp.** | especially |
| **et al.** | et alia (and others) |
| **etc.** | et cetera (and so forth) |
| **F** | Fahrenheit (scale for measuring temperature) |
| **FBI** | Federal Bureau of Investigation |
| **FYI** | for your information |
| **GOP** | Grand Old Party (Republican party) |
| **Hon.** | the Honorable |
| **HRH** | His Royal Highness, Her Royal Highness |
| **ie** | id est (that is) |
| **IQ** | intelligence quotient |
| **IRS** | Internal Revenue Service |
| **K** | 1,000 |
| **k.** | karat (unit of weight) |
| **kg** | kilogram |
| **km** | kilometer |
| **l** | liter |
| **l.** | latitude |
| **lb.** | *libra* (pound) |
| **MD** | *medicinae doctor* (doctor of medicine) |
| **mfg.** | manufacturing |
| **ml** | milliliter |
| **mm** | millimeter |
| **mph** | miles per hour |
| **ms.** | manuscript |

| | |
|---|---|
| **MSG** | monosodium glutamate (flavor enhancer) |
| **NAACP** | National Association for the Advancement of Colored People |
| **no.** | number |
| **oz.** | ounce |
| **p.** | page |
| **p.m.** | post meridiem (from noon until midnight) |
| **P.S.** | postscript |
| **pt.** | pint |
| **qt.** | quart |
| **RFD** | rural free delivery (U.S. mail category) |
| **RIP** | rest in peace |
| **RN** | registered nurse |
| **RR** | railroad |
| **RSVP** | *répondez s'il vous plaît* (French for please respond) |
| **SASE** | self-addressed, stamped envelope |
| **St.** | street, saint |
| **t.** | ton |
| **TNT** | trinitrotoluene (an explosive) |
| **UFO** | unidentified flying object |
| **UHF** | ultrahigh frequency (radio waves) |
| **v. or vs.** | versus (against) |
| **VCR** | videocassette recorder |
| **VHF** | very high frequency (radio waves) |
| **w** | watt (unit for measuring electrical power) |

# Contractions

A **contraction** is formed by putting together two words with certain letters left out. An **apostrophe** (**'**) is used in place of the missing letters.

| | | | | |
|---|---|---|---|---|
| **aren't** | are not | | **she'd** | she had/she would |
| **can't** | cannot | | **she'll** | she will |
| **couldn't** | could not | | **she's** | she is |
| **could've** | could have | | **shouldn't** | should not |
| **didn't** | did not | | **should've** | should have |
| **doesn't** | does not | | **there'd** | there had/there would |
| **don't** | do not | | **there'll** | there will |
| **hadn't** | had not | | **there's** | there is |
| **hasn't** | has not | | **they'll** | they will |
| **haven't** | have not | | **they're** | they are |
| **he'd** | he had/he would | | **'twas** | it was |
| **he'll** | he will | | **wasn't** | was not |
| **he's** | he is | | **we'll** | we will |
| **I'm** | I am | | **we're** | we are |
| **isn't** | is not | | **weren't** | were not |
| **it'd** | it had/it would | | **what'd** | what had/what would |
| **it'll** | it will | | **what's** | what is |
| **it's** | it is | | **won't** | will not |
| **let's** | let us | | **wouldn't** | would not |
| **mightn't** | might not | | **would've** | would have |
| **might've** | might have | | **you'll** | you will |
| **mustn't** | must not | | **you're** | you are |

## Chapter 1 — The Parts of a Dictionary

*Guide words usually appear in the outer corner of each page of a dictionary. The first guide word identifies the first main entry on the page. The second word identifies the last word on the page.*

*New letters break the dictionary into different sections, based on alphabetical order.*

*Pronunciation of the main entry follows the entry word or words.*

*Main entry word or words are usually set in bold type.*

*Variations in spelling follow the preferred spelling of the main entry.*

*Illustrations are used to add visual reinforcement to written definitions.*

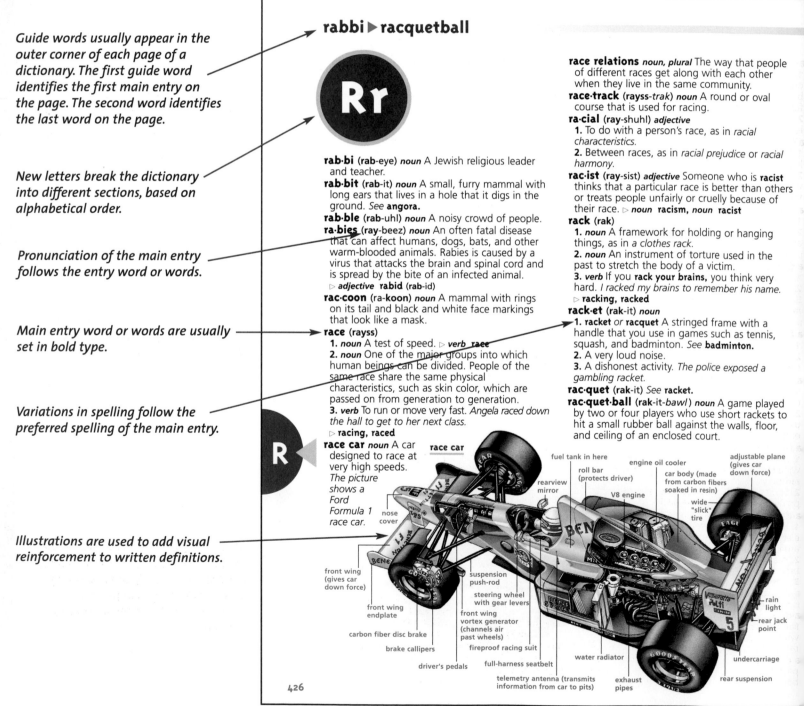

**rabbi ▶ racquetball**

**Rr**

**rab·bi** (rab-eye) *noun* A Jewish religious leader and teacher.

**rab·bit** (rab-it) *noun* A small, furry mammal with long ears that lives in a hole that it digs in the ground. *See* **angora.**

**rab·ble** (rab-uhl) *noun* A noisy crowd of people.

**ra·bies** (ray-beez) *noun* An often fatal disease that can affect humans, dogs, bats, and other warm-blooded animals. Rabies is caused by a virus that attacks the brain and spinal cord and is spread by the bite of an infected animal.
▷ *adjective* **rabid** (rab-id)

**rac·coon** (ra-koon) *noun* A mammal with rings on its tail and black and white face markings that look like a mask.

**race** (rayss)
**1.** *noun* A test of speed. ▷ *verb* **race**
**2.** *noun* One of the major groups into which human beings can be divided. People of the same race share the same physical characteristics, such as skin color, which are passed on from generation to generation.
**3.** *verb* To run or move very fast. *Angela raced down the hall to get to her next class.*
▷ **racing, raced**

**race car** *noun* A car designed to race at very high speeds. *The picture shows a Ford Formula 1 race car.*

**race relations** *noun, plural* The way that people of different races get along with each other when they live in the same community.

**race·track** (rayss-trak) *noun* A round or oval course that is used for racing.

**ra·cial** (ray-shuhl) *adjective*
**1.** To do with a person's race, as in *racial characteristics.*
**2.** Between races, as in *racial prejudice* or *racial harmony.*

**rac·ist** (ray-sist) *adjective* Someone who is **racist** thinks that a particular race is better than others or treats people unfairly or cruelly because of their race. ▷ *noun* **racism,** *noun* **racist**

**rack** (rak)
**1.** *noun* A framework for holding or hanging things, as in a *clothes rack.*
**2.** *noun* An instrument of torture used in the past to stretch the body of a victim.
**3.** *verb* If you **rack your brains,** you think very hard. *I racked my brains to remember his name.*
▷ **racking, racked**

**rack·et** (rak-it) *noun*
**1. racket** *or* **racquet** A stringed frame with a handle that you use in games such as tennis, squash, and badminton. *See* **badminton.**
**2.** A very loud noise.
**3.** A dishonest activity. *The police exposed a gambling racket.*

**rac·quet** (rak-it) *See* **racket.**

**rac·quet·ball** (rak-it-bawl) *noun* A game played by two or four players who use short rackets to hit a small rubber ball against the walls, floor, and ceiling of an enclosed court.

race car

fuel tank in here
engine oil cooler
adjustable plane (gives car down force)
roll bar (protects driver)
car body (made from carbon fibers soaked in resin)
rearview mirror
V8 engine
wide "slick" tire
nose cover
BEN
rain light
front wing (gives car down force)
suspension push-rod
rear jack point
steering wheel with gear levers
front wing endplate
front wing vortex generator (channels air past wheels)
5
carbon fiber disc brake
brake callipers
fireproof racing suit
water radiator
undercarriage
driver's pedals
full-harness seatbelt
exhaust pipes
rear suspension
telemetry antenna (transmits information from car to pits)

426

34

Parts of speech are defined for each main entry or subentry.

## radar ▶ ragweed

**ra·dar** (ray-dar) *noun*
**1.** Planes and ships use **radar** to find solid objects by reflecting radio waves off them and by receiving the reflected waves. Radar stands for *RAdio Detecting And Ranging.*
**2. radar trap** A system using radar equipment that is set up by the police to catch speeding drivers.

**ra·di·al** (ray-dee-uhl) *adjective*
**1.** Spreading out from the center or arranged like rays.
**2.** To do with a kind of automobile or truck tire whose design makes it grip the road better than traditional tires. ▷ *noun* **radial**

**ra·di·ant** (ray-dee-uhnt) *adjective*
**1.** Bright and shining.
**2.** Someone who is **radiant** looks very healthy and happy.
▷ *noun* **radiance**

**ra·di·ate** (ray-dee-*ate*) *verb*
**1.** To give off rays of light or heat.
**2.** To spread out from the center.
**3.** To send out something strongly. *Mario radiates confidence.*
▷ *verb* **radiating, radiated**

**ra·di·a·tion** (ray-dee-ay-shuhn) *noun*
**1.** The sending out of rays of light, heat, etc.
**2.** Particles that are sent out from a radioactive substance.

**ra·di·a·tor** (ray-dee-*ay*-tur) *noun*
**1.** A metal container through which hot liquid or steam circulates, sending heat into a room.
**2.** A metal device through which a liquid, usually water, circulates to cool a vehicle's engine. *See* **car, race car.**

**rad·i·cal** (rad-i-kuhl) *adjective*
**1.** If a change is **radical,** it is thorough and has a wide range of important effects. ▷ *adverb* **radically**
**2.** Someone who is **radical** believes in extreme political change. ▷ *noun* **radical**

**ra·di·o** (ray-dee-oh)
**1.** *noun* A way of communicating using electromagnetic waves broadcast from a central antenna.
**2.** *noun* A device that sends or receives these broadcasts and converts them into sound.
**3.** *verb* To send a message using a radio.
▷ **radios, radioing, radioed**
▷ *noun, plural* **radios** ▷ *adjective* **radio**

**ra·di·o·ac·tive** (ray-dee-oh-ak-tiv) *adjective*
**Radioactive** materials are made up of atoms whose nuclei break down, giving off harmful radiation. ▷ *noun* **radioactivity**

**ra·di·og·ra·phy** (ray-dee-og-ruh-fee) *noun* The process of taking X-ray photographs of people's bones, organs, etc. ▷ *noun* **radiographer**

**rad·ish** (rad-ish) *noun* A small, red and white root vegetable that you eat in salads. *See* **vegetable.**
▷ *noun, plural* **radishes**

**ra·di·um** (ray-dee-uhm) *noun* A radioactive element sometimes used to treat cancer.

**ra·di·us** (ray-dee-uhss) *noun*
**1.** A straight line segment drawn from the center of a circle to its outer edge. *See* **circle.**
**2.** The outer bone in your lower arm. *See* **skeleton.**
**3.** A circular area around a thing or a place. *Most of my friends live within a radius of one mile from my house.*
▷ *noun, plural* **radii** (ray-dee-eye)

**ra·don** (ray-don) *noun* An odorless, colorless, radioactive gas that can seep up from the earth and rocks. Radon is a chemical element produced by radium.

**raf·fle** (raf-uhl) *noun* A way of raising money by selling tickets and then giving prizes to people with winning tickets. ▷ *verb* **raffle**

**raft** (raft)
**1.** *noun* A floating platform often made from logs tied together.
**2.** *verb* To travel by raft. ▷ **rafting, rafted** ▷ *noun* **rafting**
**3.** *noun* An inflatable rubber craft with a flat bottom. *The picture shows an inflatable raft traveling through fast-moving water.*

inflatable raft

**rag** (rag)
**1.** *noun* A piece of old cloth.
**2. rags** *noun, plural* Very old, worn-out clothing.

**rage** (rayj)
**1.** *noun* Violent anger.
**2.** *verb* To be violent or noisy. *The wind raged around the house.* ▷ **raging, raged**

**rag·ged** (rag-id) *adjective* Old, torn, and worn-out. ▷ *adjective* **raggedy** ▷ *adverb* **raggedly**

**rag·time** (rag-*time*) *noun* An early style of jazz having a strong, syncopated rhythm.

**rag·weed** (rag-weed) *noun* A weed whose pollen is a cause of hay fever in the fall.

Definitions of the main entry follow the listing of pronunciation and part of speech. Definitions tell the meaning of the main entry.

Word divisions are shown in the main entry for words of one or more syllables.

Multiple definitions are provided for words with more than one meaning. The most frequently used meaning of the main entry is defined first, followed in order to the least used meaning.

R

# 2 Dictionary Notations

## Synonyms and Antonyms

**synonyms: able/strong**
Pearl is an *able* athlete and as *strong* as any member of the team.

**antonyms: able/weak**
She is an *able* student, although her eyes are so *weak* she must wear thick glasses.

**synonyms: absent/elsewhere**
The principal was *absent* because she was needed *elsewhere*.

**antonyms: absent/present**
Marcia was *absent* today, but her brother was *present* for roll call.

**synonyms: add/sum up**
I'll *add* the list and then you *sum up* to double-check me.

**antonyms: add/subtract**
When you *add* the bill, please *subtract* the credit for the CDs I returned.

# THE SECRET OF NYMS
## Synonyms and Antonyms

What is the secret of *nym*? Well, the secret is revealed in *morphemics*, the study of the meanings of units of sound (see also p. 5).

First, consider *nym*. *Nym* comes from the Greek *onoma*, meaning "name."

Next, consider the Greek words *ant* and *syn*. *Ant* means "opposite." *Syn* means "like" or "same."

Now, put *nym* together with the other words:

**Ant + (o)nym = antonym**          **A word of opposite meaning**

**Syn + (o)nym = synonym**          **A word of similar or like meaning**

## You've now discovered the secret of nym!

# Chapter 3 Pronunciation Keys

## Vowels

| a or ă | pat |
|---|---|
| ä or ah | father |
| ā or ay or a‿e | say, paid, fate |
| â(r) | air, dare |
| ar | barn |
| aw or ô | raw, ball |
| | |
| e or ĕ | men |
| ē or ee | seem |
| ēr or ihr | fear |
| | |
| i or ĭ | sit |
| ī or eye | icon (eye-kon), rye, tire |
| | |
| o or ŏ | hot |
| ō or oh | toe, tote |
| ô or or | more |
| oi | oil |
| o͝o | book |
| o͞o | ooze |
| ou | out |
| oor | poor |
| ou | out, now |
| | |
| u or ŭ | put |
| û(r) or ur | burn |
| uh | runt, comma |
| ə or uh | alone, cover, easily, scallop, minus |

## Consonants

| b | bin, cabin, cab |
|---|---|
| ch | child |
| d | do, gladden, bad |
| f | foe |
| g | go |
| h | ham, behave |
| j | jet, reject, fudge |
| k | kick, call |
| l or ll | let, will, marshmallow bundle |
| m | man, summer, him |
| n | no, banner, on |
| p | pin, super, sip |
| r | run, flurry, steer |
| s or ss | sit, misses, pass, pace |
| sh | show, fashion, bash |
| t | ten, button, sent |
| th or TH | thin, ether, with / this, wither |
| v | van, river, rove |
| w | will, away |
| wh | whale, which, nowhere |
| y | yes, onion |
| z | zoom, lazy, those |
| zh | measure, mirage |

# Acronyms

**Acronyms** are words formed from the first letters or syllables of words in phrases or titles. They are related to **abbreviations** (see pp. 31–32), the shortened versions of words or phrases. **Acronyms** don't end with periods, and are usually written in all capital letters.

| | |
|---|---|
| **AIDS** | Acquired Immune Deficiency Syndrome (disease) |
| **BASIC** | Beginner's All-purpose Symbolic Instruction Code (computer language) |
| **CARE** | Citizens for American Relief Everywhere (a relief organization) |
| **CAT scan** | Computerized Axial Tomography (medical test) |
| **DOS** | Disk Operating System (computer operation program) |
| **EPCOT** | Experimental Prototype Community of Tomorrow |
| **FICA** | Federal Insurance Contributions Act (Social Security) |
| **GATT** | General Agreement on Tariffs and Trade |
| **LASER** | Light Amplification by Stimulated Emission of Radiation |
| **loran** | long-range aid to navigation (navigation tool) |
| **MADD** | Mothers Against Drunk Driving (organization to prevent drunk driving accidents) |
| **NASA** | National Aeronautics and Space Administration (U.S. space agency) |
| **NATO** | North Atlantic Treaty Organization (peacekeeping agency) |
| **NOW** | National Organization for Women |
| **OPEC** | Organization of Petroleum Exporting Countries |
| **PIN** | Personal Identification Number (used for bank cards, credit cards, etc.) |
| **radar** | Radio Detecting And Ranging (navigation device) |
| **RAM** | Random-Access Memory (short-term computer memory) |
| **ROM** | Read-Only Memory (built-in computer memory) |
| **SADD** | Students Against Drunk Driving (organization to prevent drunk driving accidents) |
| **UNICEF** | United Nations International Children's Emergency Fund (relief organization) |
| **VISTA** | Volunteers In Service To America (helping organization) |
| **WHO** | World Health Organization |
| **ZIP code** | Zone Improvement Plan (post office delivery code) |

# Parts of Speech

## Chapter 1 Nouns

**Nouns** are words that name people, places, or things. Nouns come in many forms.

## Common and Proper Nouns

**Common** nouns are general names for people, places, and things.
**backpack, friend, holiday, mall, school, teacher, video**
**Proper** nouns are names for specific people, places, and things. Proper nouns always begin with a capital letter.

| | |
|---|---|
| **E. T.** | **Mrs. Johnson** |
| **Jackson School** | **Nintendo®** |
| **Jenny** | **Oakdale** |
| **Labor Day** | **Saturday** |

## Concrete and Abstract Nouns

**Concrete** nouns name people, places, and things that you can see, touch, taste, hear, or smell.
**fire, library, music, perfume, pizza, snow, woman**
**Abstract** nouns name ideas, feelings, or qualities.
**beauty, democracy, fairness, health, kindness, love, sadness**

> **Three little words—*a*, *an*, and *the*—mark the presence of nouns. These words are called articles. Articles are either *definite* or *indefinite*. The definite article, *the*, refers to specific or known things. The indefinite articles, *a* and *an*, refer to unspecific nouns. For example, if you are about to go on a trip, your mom will tell you to get into *the* car. Of course she means your family's car. If your older sister wants *a* big 16th birthday present, she might ask your parents for a car. This means any car, as long as it's hers.**

## Collective Nouns

**Collective** nouns name groups of people, places, or things.
**class, club, committee, humankind, orchestra**

## Compound Nouns

**Compound** nouns are made up of two or more words. Compound nouns can be **common**, **proper**, **singular**, **plural**, **concrete**, **abstract**, or **collective**. They can be one word, two words, or hyphenated.
**baseball, daydreams, electric guitar, jack-o'-lantern**

# Singular and Plural Nouns

*Singular* nouns name only one person, place, or thing. *Plural* nouns name more than one person, place, or thing.

# Possessive Nouns

A *possessive* noun tells who or what owns something.

**The girl's desk was messy.**                    **Jeff's ball is new.**

To make singular nouns possessive, add **'s** to the end of most nouns.

| | |
|---|---|
| **cat** | **the cat's toy** |
| **Robert** | **Robert's spelling test** |
| **Tess** | **Tess's notebook** |

To make plural nouns possessive, add an apostrophe (**'**) to the end of the noun when the plural noun ends in **s**.

| | |
|---|---|
| **cats** | **the cats' scratching posts** |
| **students** | **the students' music teacher** |
| **teachers** | **the teachers' lounge** |

If the last letter of the plural noun does not end in **s**, add **'s** to form the plural possessive.

| | |
|---|---|
| **children** | **the children's toys** |
| **people** | **the people's choice** |
| **geese** | **the geese's flight pattern** |

# Making a Singular Noun Plural

1. Add an **-s** to the end of most singular nouns to make them plural.

    **dog + s = dogs    cat + s = cats    test + s = tests**

2. Add **-es** to the end of a singular noun ending in **ch**, **s**, **sch**, **sh**, **x**, or **z** to make it plural.

    **dress + es = dresses   lunch + es = lunches   quiz + es = quizzes**

3. Change **f** to **v** and add **-es** to the end of most singular nouns ending in **f**, **lf**, or **fe** to make them plural. There are exceptions to this rule!

    **knife/knives    leaf/leaves    life/lives**

    **exceptions:    sniff/sniffs   safe/safes**

4. Drop the **y** and add **-ies** to a singular noun ending in a consonant followed by **y** to make it plural.

    **fly/flies    battery/batteries    penny/pennies**

5. Add an **-s** to a singular noun ending in a vowel followed by **y** to make it plural.

    **day/days    key/keys    boy/boys**

6. Add **-es** to most words ending in **o** preceded by a consonant to make them plural.

    **potato/potatoes    echo/echoes    tomato/tomatoes**

7. Add an **-s** after the most important word in a hyphenated compound noun or to one written as two words to make it plural.

    **brother-in-law/brothers-in-law    computer drive/computer drives**

8. Memorize odd plurals.

    **man/men    woman/women    goose/geese    foot/feet**

#  Chapter 2 Pronouns

*Pronouns* are words that can be substituted for nouns in naming people, places, and things.

## Personal and Possessive Pronouns

*Personal pronouns* refer to people or animals.

**I, you, he, she, it, we, they, me, him, her, us, them**
**They told us that they were going to meet her at the mall.**

Sometimes personal pronouns are used to show possession or ownership. These personal pronouns are sometimes called *possessive pronouns.*

**my, mine, your(s), his, her(s), its, our(s), their(s), whose**
**If this bubble gum isn't hers, then it must be mine.**

> **Never use an apostrophe in a possessive pronoun!**

# PRESTO, CHANGE-O:
## Substituting Pronouns for Nouns

### SUBJECT PRONOUNS

*Subject pronouns* are often used with a noun or another pronoun as part of the subject of a clause or sentence (see pp. 56–59).

**These and those are very different.**
**She and I went to the movies last Saturday.**
**Some had a great time at the party. Others did not.**

### OBJECT PRONOUNS

*Object* or *predicate pronouns* are often used with a noun or another pronoun as part of the direct object (see Subjects and Predicates, p. 56).

**Fred saw him at the fair.**
**We share the dog. It belongs to her and me.**
**Always speak of yourself last.**

41

# Demonstrative Pronouns

*Demonstrative pronouns* refer to specific people, places, or things.

**this, that, these, those**

**Which ice skates are lighter, these or those?**

# Indefinite Pronouns

*Indefinite pronouns* refer to or replace nouns in a general way. Some indefinite pronouns are also used as adjectives. They are then followed by a noun, as in *both cats* or *each flower*. Examples follow:

**all, any, anyone, both, each, either, every, many, neither, nobody, no one, nothing, other(s), several, some, someone.**

**Anyone can try out for the team, but only some will make it.**

# Reflexive Pronouns

*Reflexive pronouns* are used to refer back to subject nouns and pronouns.

**myself, yourself, himself, herself, itself, ourselves, yourselves, themselves**

**Cathy knew she could do it herself.**

# Intensive Pronouns

*Intensive pronouns* are reflexive pronouns that emphasize a noun or another pronoun.

**John himself, she herself, the team themselves**

**We ourselves formed the new reading club.**

# Interrogative Pronouns

*Interrogative pronouns* are pronouns used to ask questions.

**what, which, who, whom, whose**

**What is happening and to whom?**

# Chapter 3 Verbs

*Verbs* are words that describe an action or a state of being.

## Action and Linking Verbs

*Action verbs* describe activity. Action can be physical.

**eat, leap, read, run, sleep, swim, walk, yell**
**Abe Lincoln walked seven miles to school every day.**

Action can also mean quieter activities.

**care, concentrate, forgive, grow, hate, love, think**
**A tree grows in Brooklyn.**

*Linking verbs* do not describe an action, but a state of being. They connect a noun or an adjective to the subject of a clause or sentence.

**Jose was happy.**
**The plan looks good.**

# Helping Verbs

*Helping verbs* help the main verb describe action that happened in the past, is happening in the present, or will happen in the future. There are 23 helping verbs.

| | | | | |
|---|---|---|---|---|
| am | can | had | might | were |
| are | could | has | must | will |
| be | did | have | shall | would |
| been | do | is | should | |
| being | does | may | was | |

A main verb can have up to three helping verbs.

**The bus is coming at three o'clock.**

**Oops! The bus must have gone at 2:55.**

**We could have gone on the bus if you hadn't forgotten your backpack in your locker.**

# Infinitive Form

An *infinitive* is a main verb usually preceded by the word *to*. It does the work of both a verb and a noun, and it may be used as an adjective or adverb.

*noun*

To go often is her goal.     *verb*

I like to play the piano.

A desire to study often brings success in school.

*adjective*

# Verb Tenses

The *tense* of a verb tells you the time the action takes place or the state of being—past, present, or future. There are six main tenses:

**1 Present tense. The present tense means now.**
The dog *has* fleas.
I *go* to school every day.

**2 Past tense. The past tense means before now.**
The dog *had* fleas until he had a flea shampoo.
I *went* to school last week.

**3 Future tense. The future tense means not yet.**
The dog *will have* fleas if he sleeps in the barn.
I *will go* to school next Monday.

**4 Present perfect tense. The present perfect tense means started in the past and continuing up to the present.**
The dog *has had* fleas for three years.
I *have gone* to school on the bus for years.

**5 Past perfect tense. The past perfect tense means finished before some other past action.**
The dog *had had* fleas for two years before he stopped scratching.
I *had gone* to fourth grade before I started fifth grade.

**6 Future perfect tense. The future perfect tense means action will start and finish in the future.**
The vet *will have given* all the puppies a flea collar two months after they are born.
I *will have gone* to school for three months before we get a break.

# Participles

A **participle** is a form of a verb that can be used as a verb or as an adjective. There are two kinds of participles — present and past.

**Present participles usually end in -ing and follow the helping verbs for to be (see p. 43).**
**Jeff is going to be George Washington in the school pageant.**
**Amy will be playing Martha Washington.**
**Past participles usually end in -ed or -en, or -d, -t, or -n, and follow the helping verbs have or had.**
**Rowan had decided to try out for band instead of the pageant.**
**Marty and Courtney have been chosen for the parts of John and Abigail Adams.**

# Principal Parts of Verbs

Each verb has four main parts, called **principal parts**.
The principal parts include:

1. **The infinitive**
   to swim, to run, to throw
2. **The past tense**
   swam, ran, threw
3. **The present participle**
   (to be) swimming, (to be) running, (to be) throwing
4. **The past participle**
   (have/had) swum, (have/has) run, (have/had) thrown

# Regular and Irregular Verbs

**Regular verbs** are verbs that can be changed from the present to the past and past participle simply by adding **-ed** or **-d**.
**Now I jump. Yesterday I jumped. I have jumped.**
**Now we skate. Yesterday we skated. I have skated.**
The past tense and past participles of irregular verbs are formed in unpredictable ways.
**You do what you like. I did my homework, and Ian has done his.**

## To Be or Not to Be

The verb **to be** is the most often used verb in the English language. It is an irregular verb. In fact, there are eight different words in the verb to be.
**is, am, are, was, were, be, being, been**
**Now I am. Yesterday I was. I have been.**
**Now we are. Yesterday we were. We have been.**
**Just being here is great!**

# Adjectives

**Adjectives** are words that describe nouns and pronouns. Adjectives **modify**, or tell more about, nouns. They answer one of three questions:

**What kind?**
Eric watched the magnificent eagle soar through the sky.

**How many?**
Katie checked out eight books from the library.

**Which one(s)?**
Ben took that route to the farm.

# Common Adjectives

**Common adjectives** describe nouns in a general way. These adjectives tell just about anything, from size, shape, and number to color, design, and character.

**big, friendly, green, round, spotted, nine**
**The big dog growled at me.**
**The friendly dog doesn't growl.**
**Nine dogs can make a lot of noise.**

# Proper Adjectives

**Proper adjectives** are formed from proper nouns. They are always capitalized.

**America/American, Asia/Asian, Queen Victoria/Victorian**
**I love American music.**
**We have Asian students from China, Japan, and Thailand.**
**That Victorian house looks haunted.**

# Demonstrative Adjectives

**Demonstrative adjectives** are the same words as demonstrative pronouns (see p. 42). As adjectives, they go with nouns and answer the question "Which one(s)?".

**that, these, this, those**
**That movie was great, but those songs were awful.**
**This candy tastes good, but these peanuts are rotten.**

# Using Adjectives to Compare

Comparisons can be made on three levels, or **degrees** — positive, comparative, and superlative.

**1** **The positive degree describes one thing.**
Kyle was *good* at solving riddles.
Kyle is *short*.

**2** **The comparative degree compares two things.**
Kyle's sister was *better* than he.
Kyle's sister is *shorter*.

**3** **The superlative degree compares three or more things.**
Kyle's brother was the *best* riddle solver of all.
Kyle's brother is *shortest*.

To compare adjectives (and adverbs, see p. 48):

**1** **Add -er and -est to most adjectives that are one or two syllables long.**
big/bigger/biggest   strong/stronger/strongest

**2** **If the one- or two-syllable adjective ends in y, drop the y and add -ier and -iest.**
happy/happier/happiest   homely/homelier/homeliest   silly/sillier/silliest

**3** **Use more and most or less and least in front of most adjectives with two or more syllables.**
advanced/more advanced/most advanced   capable/more capable/most capable

**4** **Add -r and -st to short adjectives that end in e.**
little/littler/littlest   subtle/subtler/subtlest   able/abler/ablest

**5** **Some adjectives are irregular and don't follow these rules, for example:**
bad/worse/worst   good/better/best

# Adverbs

*Adverbs* describe verbs, adjectives, or other adverbs. Adverbs are used to make meanings clearer or more exact.

## Adverbs and Verbs

Adverbs answer four questions about the verbs they describe — how, when, where, and to what extent?

**The young girl jumped high. She danced beautifully.**
**The tall boy came late. He apologized immediately.**
**The dog barked loudly when he was here. The child sat there.**
**The elderly man swam daily. He enjoyed it thoroughly.**

## Adverbs and Adjectives

Adverbs usually answer the question "How?" when they describe adjectives.

**The very young girl danced beautifully.**
**The extremely tall boy came late.**
**The annoyingly noisy dog barked loudly.**
**The exceptionally elderly man swam daily.**

## Adverbs and Adverbs

Adverbs answer the questions "How?" or "How much?" when they describe other adverbs.

**The young girl jumped exceptionally high.**
**The tall boy came very late.**
**The noisy dog barked really loudly.**
**The elderly man swam amazingly fast.**

## Comparing Adverbs

Adverbs can be compared, just like adjectives, by using the positive, comparative, and superlative degrees (see p. 47).

**I run fast enough to make the track team, but Amy runs faster, and Tamika runs fastest.**

# A WHOLE NEW WORD:
## MAKING ADVERBS FROM ADJECTIVES

Many adjectives can be changed into adverbs by adding **-ly** to the end.

**loud/loudly, quick/quickly, bad/badly**

But this magic doesn't apply to the three most common adverbs in the English language: ***not***, ***very***, and ***too***.

# Chapter 6

# Prepositions

A **preposition** relates a noun or pronoun to another word in the same sentence. A preposition can also connect a pronoun to a noun in a sentence. A preposition usually tells where something is, where something is going, or when something is happening. A preposition always introduces a phrase. The noun at the end of the prepositional phrase is the **object of the preposition** (see also p. 54).

> **The cups are over the sink.**
> **Lee went to the concert with Kim.**
> **Mary ran to her mother.**
> **The cat ran after the mouse.**

## List of Common One-, Two-, and Three-Word Prepositions

| | | |
|---|---|---|
| about | but | off |
| above | by | on |
| according to | despite | on account of |
| across | down | onto |
| after | due to | out |
| against | during | out of |
| ahead of | except | outside |
| along | except for | over |
| along with | for | past |
| among | from | since |
| around | in | through |
| as | in addition to | throughout |
| as for | in back of | to |
| as to | in case of | toward |
| at | in front of | under |
| away from | in regard to | underneath |
| because of | inside | until |
| before | in spite of | up |
| behind | instead of | upon |
| below | into | up to |
| beside | like | with |
| between | near | within |
| beyond | of | without |

(See also Prepositional Phrases, p. 54.)

above

over

in

inside     upon

behind

alongside

below

under

50

# Chapter 7 Conjunctions

*Conjunctions* are words that join words, phrases, clauses, and sentences.

## Coordinating Conjunctions

*Coordinating conjunctions* join words, phrases, and sentences.

and, but, nor, so, or, yet

The kids came late and baked a cake.

I went to the ballpark but the game was canceled.

I have a sled yet it never snows here.

I can neither eat nor drink before I play soccer.

## Subordinating Conjunctions

*Subordinating conjunctions* join dependent clauses to independent clauses.

after, although, as, as if, because, before, for, if,
once, since, so, so that, than, that, though, till,
unless, until, when, whenever, where, whereas, wherever,
whether, while

Father came home after the work was done.

We were happy once the ice cream was served.

Daniel practiced his music so that he could try out for band.

I cannot go until she comes.

51

# Correlative Conjunctions

*Correlative conjunctions* are always used in pairs in a phrase or sentence even though they are split up by other words.

both/and, either/or, neither/nor, not only/but also, whether/or

The hungry elephant ate not only the pretzels but also the peanuts.

You should have given him either the pretzels or the peanuts.

Yes, but he wanted to have both the pretzels and the peanuts.

# Adverbial Conjunctions

*Adverbial conjunctions* join clauses or sentences of equal importance.

accordingly, besides, consequently, furthermore, hence, however, likewise, moreover, nevertheless, so, still, therefore, thus

The pretzel bag was left open; consequently, the pretzels went stale.

My dog doesn't like peanuts; however, he loves peanut butter!

I think, therefore I am.

# Chapter 8 Interjections

**Interjections** are words, phrases, and nonsense words that express strong feelings. Interjections are **interjected** into, or interrupt, a smooth flow of thoughts to emphasize certain feelings, for example, excitement, happiness, sadness, fear, or anger. Interjections stand apart from sentences and are usually punctuated with exclamation points (see p. 62).

**aha, ahem, alas, all right, eureka, gracious, hello, help, hey, oh, oops, ouch, phew, thanks, ugh, well, wow, yikes, yippee, yuck**

**Aha!  I've caught you!**

**Oops!  You put the coin in the wrong slot.**

**Yuck!  What a mess!**

# 9 Phrases, Clauses, and Sentences

Some words convey powerful emotion or action just by themselves. But most words need to be combined with other words to get your message across.

## Phrases

**Phrases** are any groups of two or more words that together form a thought or express one meaning. A phrase has no subject or verb. There are four basic types of phrases: prepositional, participial, infinitive and gerund, and verb phrases.

### PREPOSITIONAL PHRASES

**Prepositional phrases** are groups of two or more words that begin with a preposition and end with a noun or pronoun. The noun or pronoun is known as the **object of the preposition**.

**after the hour** ←

**around the world** ←

**throughout the day** ←            *object of the preposition*

**to them** ←

A pronoun immediately following a preposition is always the object of the preposition.

**after her**
**by us**
**without them**

### PARTICIPIAL PHRASES

**Participial phrases** are groups of two or more words that begin with **participles** (see p. 45).

**writing a book**
**grasping his sword**
**leaping to my feet**

## INFINITIVE AND GERUND PHRASES

**Infinitive phrases** are groups of two or more words consisting of an infinitive verb or an infinitive verb plus an adverb. Infinitive verbs are easily identified. They begin with the word **to**.

**to go**
**to go boldly**
**to play**
**to care deeply**

**Gerund phrases** are groups of two or more words that contain a gerund. A gerund is a verb form that ends in **-ing** and acts as a noun.

**my being there**
**his going to the moon**
**your wanting a new skateboard**

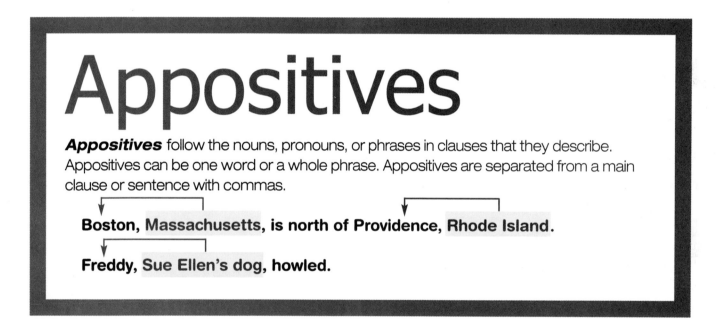

# Appositives

**Appositives** follow the nouns, pronouns, or phrases in clauses that they describe. Appositives can be one word or a whole phrase. Appositives are separated from a main clause or sentence with commas.

**Boston, Massachusetts, is north of Providence, Rhode Island.**

**Freddy, Sue Ellen's dog, howled.**

## VERB PHRASES

**Verb phrases** are groups of two or more verbs that describe an action. They are made up of a main verb and one or more helping verbs.

**have come**
**had gone**
**will be coming**
**would have come**
**should be going**

(See also Participles, p. 45.)

# Clauses

*Clauses* are groups of two or more words that have a **subject** and a **predicate**. Clauses are either **principal** or **subordinate**.

## PRINCIPAL CLAUSES

*Principal clauses* are also called **independent**, or **main**, **clauses**. Only principal clauses can stand alone as complete **sentences** (see pp. 57–59).

**The dog was sick.**
**The dog ate grass, and the cat licked her paws.**

## SUBORDINATE CLAUSES

*Subordinate clauses* are also called **dependent clauses**. Subordinate clauses express ideas or information related to principal clauses.

**The dog was sick because he ate grass.**
**The cat licked her paws after she played with the yarn.**

---

**Subordinate clauses cannot stand alone as sentences. They are combined with principal clauses to complete thoughts or give greater meaning to a sentence.**

---

# Subjects and Predicates:
## Simple, Complete, and Compound

A *simple subject* is the noun or pronoun that tells who or what a clause or sentence is about.

**The boy played soccer.**

A *complete subject* is the noun plus any descriptive word or phrase that goes with it.

**The athletic boy on the football field played soccer.**

A *compound subject* is two or more simple subjects joined by a conjunction (see p. 51).

**My mother and I watched the boy play soccer.**

A *simple predicate* is just the verb in the predicate.

**The horse whinnied.**

A *complete predicate* is the verb plus any descriptive words or phrases that make up the predicate. It is everything in a clause or sentence that is not contained in the complete subject.

**The horse whinnied loudly at the trainer.**

A *compound predicate* is found in sentences where two or more different actions are described.

**The horse whinnied and snorted.**

# Sentences

***Sentences*** are groups of words that express a complete thought. You can make a sentence by putting together a noun (subject) and a verb (predicate).

Sentences can be short or long, simple or complicated. But all sentences fall into one of three categories:  simple, compound, or complex.

| Noun (subject) | Verb (predicate) |
|---|---|
| I | go. |
| He | runs. |
| Mosquitoes | bite. |
| People | care. |

## SIMPLE SENTENCES

A ***simple sentence*** is made up of one **subject** and one **predicate**.
   **The boys played baseball.**
   **The boys played baseball against the girls' team.**
   **The boys from Middletown played against the Hightown girls' team.**

## COMPOUND SENTENCES

A **compound sentence** is made up of two or more simple sentences joined by a conjunction (see pp. 51–52).

> The girls played baseball **and** they beat the other team.
>
> I go to the playground with my brother every day, **but** yesterday he wouldn't play with me.
>
> I like broccoli raw **yet** I can't eat it cooked.

I won't play.

## COMPLEX SENTENCES

A **complex sentence** is made up of a principal clause and one or more subordinate clauses.

> Fighting infection was difficult until penicillin was discovered.
>
> When I forgot my lunch, I had to eat that gross cafeteria food.
>
> The fifth graders left the playground early because it started to rain.

# Four Types of Sentences

## DECLARATIVE SENTENCES

*Declarative sentences* make statements.

**Life is good.**

**I am happy, and you are sad.**

**You ate an extra scoop of ice cream.**

## INTERROGATIVE SENTENCES

*Interrogative sentences* ask questions.

**Is life good?**

**Are you happy, too?**

**Did your stomach hurt after you ate the fifth
scoop of ice cream?**

## IMPERATIVE SENTENCES

*Imperative sentences* give commands or request action.

**Go.**

**Open the door, and go inside.**

**After you open the door, go inside.**

## EXCLAMATORY SENTENCES

*Exclamatory sentences* express strong feelings or emotions.
They end in exclamation points (see p. 62) instead of periods.

**I feel horrible!**

**I ate a whole pizza and I'm still hungry!**

**I studied hard, so I got the highest score on the test!**

# You Understood

*Imperative sentences* often don't have subjects — or
do they? When you give a command, you are addressing
someone else. He or she knows whom you're talking to.
The **you** is the subject, and whether or not you say it, **you** is
understood.

**(You) Leave my cat alone.**

**(You) Go.**

# PUNCTUATION MARKS
## and Some of Their Uses

### Apostrophe (')

**1. Shows possession**

> Jamai's shoe, the girls' toys, Mary's and John's boats

**2. Shows contractions**

> can't, she's, would've, '98

**3. Creates plurals of lowercase letters**

> a's, b's, c's

---

### Colon (:)

**1. Introduces lists**

> The clock has three parts: a face, a dial, and numbers.

**2. Introduces excerpts and long quotations**

> As Lincoln wrote in his Gettysburg Address:
> "Fourscore and seven years ago, our fathers brought forth on this continent a new nation, conceived in liberty, and dedicated to the proposition that all men are created equal."

**3. Separates hours from minutes when writing time in numerals**

> 2:00, 4:15, 8:55

**4. Punctuates the greeting in a formal letter**

> Dear Ms. President:

---

### Comma (,)

**1. Separates clauses in sentences, including long compound sentences**

> The rain came, which was very good for the crops.

**2. Separates items in a series**

> I want a baseball, a glove, and a bat for my birthday.

**3. Separates three or more adjectives in a series**

> I saw red, green, yellow, and orange kites.

**4. Separates a direct quotation in a sentence**

> Marty said, "Get out of there!"

**5. Separates a city from a state**

  Minneapolis, Minnesota

**6. Separates the month and day from the year in a date**

  June 6, 2005

**7. Sets apart mild interjections from the rest of a sentence**

  Gosh, I was hungry.

**8. Sets apart appositives**

  Bill, my brother, was late.

**9. Punctuates the greeting and closing in a friendly letter**

  Dear Sally,
  Your friend,

---

## Dash (—)

**1. Works like a comma to separate phrases or clauses in a sentence**

  President Clinton — along with many others — studied law before entering politics.

**2. Works like a colon to separate lists**

  I had three choices — stand, run, or sit.

**3. Works like an ellipsis to show interrupted or unfinished statements**

  I would never have guessed, but then —

**4. Works like a comma to separate appositives**

  My father — a great guy — built a boxcar for the derby.

---

## Ellipsis ( . . . )

**1. Replaces words left out in the middle of a quote or obvious text**

  I pledge allegiance to . . . America.

**2. Shows that a thought or list should continue in the same pattern**

  A is for apple, b is for box, c is for cow . . .

**3. A period followed by three ellipsis points shows that words have been left out at the end of a sentence, paragraph, or longer piece of writing.**

  I pledge allegiance to the flag. . . .

## Exclamation point (!)

**1. Ends exclamatory sentences**
   I won!

**2. Separates an interjection from a sentence**
   Hooray! I won!

**3. Ends strong imperative sentences**
   Get away from the fire!

---

## Hyphen (-)

**1. Connects two-part words**
   roly-poly, twenty-two, air-conditioning

**2. Separates words into syllables**
   ap-ple

**3. Connects compound nouns and adjectives**
   well-known man, teacher-in-training

**4. Separates some prefixes**
   ex-champion, re-create

**5. Divides words at the end of a line of writing**
   diction-      nota-
   ary           tion

---

## Parentheses ( )

**1. Hold additional information in a sentence, but information that is not necessary to include in the sentence**
   I'll tell you (and you can listen to) my story.
   The girl was born (two weeks early) in Florida.

**2. Hold explanatory information or alternative spellings, names, or symbols**
   The gorgon (a mythical monster) frightened the sailors.
   The price was stated as fifteen dollars ($15).

## Period (.)

**1. Ends a declarative sentence**

I will go to the zoo today.

**2. Follows most initials**

John F. Kennedy was a popular president.

**3. Follows most abbreviations**

The giraffe was 12 ft. tall.

**4. Follows numerals when writing lists**

1. Trading Cards

2. Bubble Gum, etc.

3. Milk

## Question mark (?)

**1. Ends an interrogative sentence**

What are you doing up there?

**2. Shows doubt or uncertainty when written in parentheses**

King Tut lived 3,000 (?) years ago.

## Quotation marks (" ")

**1. Show a person's exact words**

The teacher said, "Start writing."

**2. Set apart titles of articles in magazines and newspapers**

Did you read the story "Amazing Facts" in Sunday's paper?

**3. Set apart chapter titles in books as well as essay, short story, song, and poem titles**

"Getting Started" is the title of the first chapter of *Building a Treehouse*.

**4. Set apart special words and phrases, including slang, nonstandard English, and technical words**

The answer to the clue "fruity" was the word "apple."

**5. When single ('/'), show a quotation within another quotation**

"The teacher said, 'You kids are too much,' when we locked the classroom door," Fred explained to the principal.

## Semicolon (;)

**1. Joins related independent clauses into one sentence when they are not joined by a conjunction**

> The Great Houdini died; he could not make his greatest escape.

**2. Sets apart items in a list, particularly items following a colon**

> This is what we need to do for the party: send the invitations; bake the cake; buy the candles, paper plates, napkins, and forks; and reserve the party room.

---

## Underline (_____)

**1. Sets apart book, movie, play, opera, TV show, and video titles**

> Have you read <u>Little House on the Prairie</u>?

**2. Sets apart the names of newspapers and magazines**

> I read the article in <u>Junior Scholastic</u>.

**3. Sets apart foreign words and phrases**

> <u>Adiós</u>, my good friends.

**4. Adds emphasis to words and phrases**

> She told us <u>never</u> to eat with our hands.
> He mentioned <u>a long time ago</u> that he would be going.

Note: In typeset books or on a word processor, italic type (or *italics*) is used in place of underlining. Italic type looks a little like cursive handwriting. In this book's typeface, *italic type looks like this.*

# Sentence Diagrams

**Sentence diagrams** illustrate how parts of speech work to form complete thoughts or **sentences** (see also p. 57). Sentence diagrams also show the main parts of a sentence and the words and phrases that are added to communicate greater detail or more precise information.

Life is good.

You ate an extra scoop of ice cream.

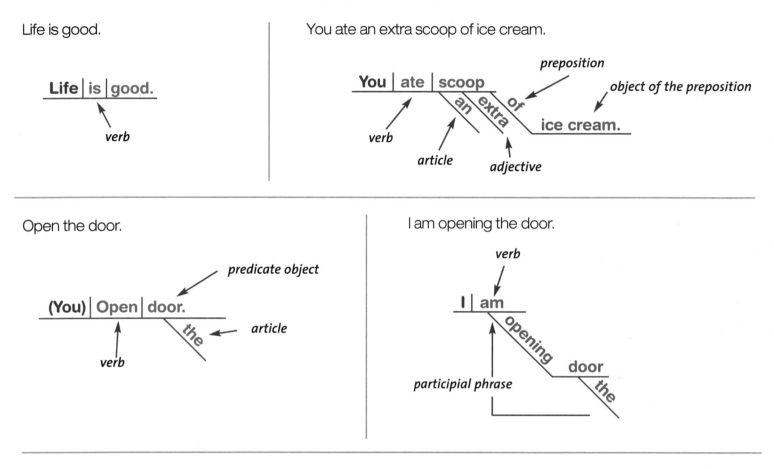

Open the door.

I am opening the door.

Yes, the hungry elephant ate not only pretzels but also peanuts.

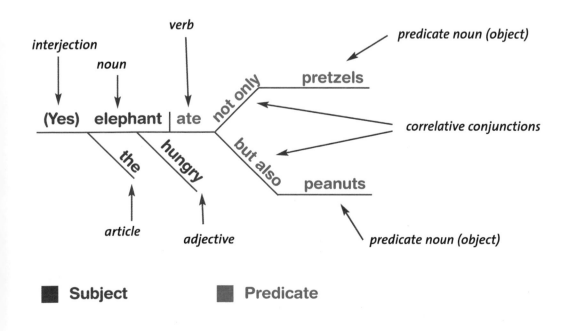

█ **Subject**      █ **Predicate**

# Chapter 10

# Combining Sentences to Make Paragraphs

**Paragraphs** are groups of sentences that describe related ideas. A good paragraph includes the following: a topic sentence, detail sentences, proper order, and a consistent theme. In practical writing (see pp. 98–111), the sentences within a paragraph combine to develop the ideas and point of view of the writing. In creative writing (see pp. 88–97), sentences combine into paragraphs to flesh out essential details of the story, such as character description, setting, dialogue, and theme (see also p. 93).

## Topic Sentences

The **topic sentence** states the theme or main idea of a paragraph. It is usually the first sentence of a paragraph, but it can also be found at the end. A topic sentence is almost never found in the middle of a paragraph.

## Detail Sentences

**Detail sentences** tell more about the main idea of the paragraph.

## Order of Sentences

The **order of sentences** is important in writing good paragraphs. For example, if you wrote a paragraph explaining the four steps in flossing your teeth, you wouldn't start by writing, "Throw away the used dental floss." Order should always make sense.

## Theme

The **theme**, or main idea, holds together all the sentences in a paragraph. It is stated in the topic sentence. Be sure all the detail sentences stick to the theme and tell about the main idea. Sentences that do not belong upset the sense or flow in the order of the sentences. The sentences that don't make sense are called **non sequiturs**, or ideas that "don't follow."

## Different Paragraphs for Different Purposes: Chronological, Cause and Effect, and Compare and Contrast

Paragraphs can be constructed for different purposes. When they are used to describe sequences and time frames, they are **chronological paragraphs**. Some paragraphs describe events and what happens after they occur. These paragraphs describe **cause and effect**. Still other paragraphs are organized to point out similarities and differences in two or more things. These paragraphs **compare and contrast**.

Writing in chronological, cause and effect, and compare and contrast forms isn't simply used to organize sentences within paragraphs, however. These forms are also used to organize essays and other longer pieces of practical writing (see p. 98).

Topic Sentence. Remember, the topic sentence states the theme of the paragraph. It is usually the first sentence.

Growing orange plants is as easy as one-two-three. First save the seeds from the next orange you eat. Next, place the seeds about one inch apart on top of a container filled with potting soil. Last, cover with about a quarter inch of additional potting soil, water, and wait. If you keep your container in a sunny place and make sure the soil stays moist, your orange seeds should sprout in two to three weeks.

Detail Sentences. In this paragraph, the writer tells more about growing orange plants.

Order of Sentences. In order to make sense, the detail sentences must follow a logical order or sequence. Imagine rewriting the paragraph starting with the third sentence. It would make no sense.

# Chapter 1 Outlines and Story Maps

## Outlines: Skeletons for Organized Writers

**Outlines** are tools that are used in the planning stages of writing, sometimes called **prewriting**. Outlines help you organize ideas for a school report or a speech. If you have a hard time getting all your ideas into an outline, it may mean you have chosen too large a topic. For example, it you are reporting on a trip to the zoo, you might find it easier to write about one of the exhibits or one zoo activity rather than try to describe every exhibit that you visited or every animal that you saw. A story on big cats or feeding time will allow you to say a lot on one interesting subject.

> **Outlines include three basic elements: a title, main headings, and subheadings. Together these elements help you create logical beginnings, middles, and endings for your work. Outlines also help you decide where it makes sense to include the information you want.**

Bats ←

> **TITLE**
> *The **title** should tell the subject of the work. The title of the outline may or may not become the title of the paper.*

I. The Body
 A. Wings
  1. Only mammal that can fly
   a. They fly more slowly than most birds
   b. They can fly through tiny gaps and holes

2. The wings contract and fold along the bones when bats aren't flying

B. Head and Body
   1. Strange face, sometimes really scary or ugly looking
   2. Huge ears
   3. Legs, but no arms—only wings
   4. Sleep upside down
C. Senses
   1. Almost blind
   2. Echolocation
      a. Produce high-pitched sound
      b. Sound works like radar to help bat locate food or obstacles

**MAIN HEADINGS**
*Main headings* state the main topics covered in the paper. The first is the opening paragraph, and the last is the conclusion. You can include as few as two other main headings or as many as you need to cover your subject. To show main headings, use a capital Roman numeral and a period.

II. Eating Habits
   A. Most eat insects
   B. Mice or other bats
   C. Flower nectar
   D. Fruit

III. Life Cycle and Habitat
   A. Live up to 20 years
   B. Live birth, usually one baby at a time
   C. Live almost anywhere in the world
      1. Not in extremely cold places
      2. Not on some islands
   D. Some species migrate to find food
   E. Species in cold climates hibernate in winter

**SUBHEADINGS**
*Subheadings* come under main headings. For the first level of subheadings, use capital letters. For the second level of subheadings, use Arabic numerals.

# Story Maps: The Path of Fiction

**Story maps** or **plans** are outlines for fiction writers. You can "map" the main parts of stories or plays: setting, characters, major events, problems (challenges), and solutions.

Story maps can be laid out in many different ways. Unlike outlines, you don't have to give the map a title or use Roman numerals. But, to be useful, the maps should include all the main parts of the story or play. These main parts should be organized around a **plot** (see p. 81), or action line.

# Story Map

Title: _Canine Crusader_   Author: _Kendra Leigh Ealy_

Characters: Homer (the dog), Sally, Mom, Dad, Zorch (a dog) Mr. Grumpy, and the dog from the vacant lot
Place: Sunnyglade, USA
Time: The present

Problem: Someone was stealing Milky Bones from all the neighbors' houses, and everyone thought it was the new dog, Zorch.

Events Leading to Resolution:

Zorch and his family move into Sally's neighborhood.

Homer, Sally's dog, makes friends with Zorch.

Milky Bones start disappearing.

Zorch gets stuck under Mr. Grumpy's picket fence, right next to a pile of Milky Bones.

Resolution: Homer proves Zorch is innocent. He takes Sally through the neighborhood to the vacant lot; there, a little dog, dirty and hungry, is asleep on a bed of old Milky Bone bags. Sally and Homer bring the poor pup home to live, and the Milky Bones no longer disappear.

# Circle Story Framework

Use a *circle story framework* to establish *sequence*, or the order of events in your story.

Sally and Homer like to play together.

Zorch likes to play with Sally and Homer.

Homer and Zorch learn from Sally about the mystery of the Milky Bones.

Homer and Zorch attempt to solve the mystery.

Zorch gets stuck in Mr. Grumpy's fence (while chasing after Homer and the dog from the vacant lot).

Homer takes Sally to vacant lot - clears Zorch's name, and adopts little dog.

# Flow Chart

A *flow chart* and a *time line* can be used much the same way as a *circle story framework*.

Sally and Homer like to play together.

Homer and Zorch attempt to solve the mystery.

Zorch likes to play with Sally and Homer.

Zorch gets stuck in Mr. Grumpy's fence (while chasing Homer).

Homer and Zorch learn from Sally about the mystery of the Milky Bones.

Homer takes Sally to vacant lot—clears Zorch's name, and adopts little dog.

# Time Line

| | |
|---|---|
| **1a** | Sally and Homer like to play together. |
| **1b** | Zorch likes to play with Sally and Homer. |
| **2** | Homer and Zorch learn from Sally about the mystery of the Milky Bones. |
| **3** | Homer and Zorch attempt to solve the mystery. |
| **4** | Zorch gets stuck in Mr. Grumpy's fence (while chasing after Homer and the dog from the vacant lot). |
| **5** | Homer takes Sally to vacant lot - clears Zorch's name, and adopts little dog. |

# Cause/Effect Diagram

**Effect:**

Neighbors are upset — want to find thief.

**Cause:**

Neighbor's Milky Bones are missing.

**Cause:**

Milky Bones are stolen.

**Effect:**

Sally tells Homer and Zorch.

**Cause:**

Zorch is new dog in town.

**Effect:**

Zorch is blamed for stealing Milky Bones.

**Effect:**

Homer and Zorch attempt to solve crime.

**Cause:**

Milky Bones found near hole in vacant lot.

# Venn Diagram

Use **Venn diagrams** to compare two or more characters or events.

Homer

Zorch

- Basset Hound
- good sniffer
- bad listener
- well-known in the neighborhood

- live in same neighborhood
- loved
- like playing hide-n-seek

- Black Lab
- not a great sniffer
- good listener
- doesn't know neighborhood

- like Milky Bones

- know vacant lot

- aren't known in the neighborhood

- no family to love
- no regular meals

Dog from Vacant Lot

# Chapter 2

# Rough Draft to Final Copy

Once you've prepared an *outline* or a *story map*, you're ready to write the **rough** or **first draft**. The rough draft is also called **sloppy copy**.

Rough drafts help you organize your ideas into sentences. They also help show how the different parts of your writing fit together. The rough draft can be written in pen or pencil on paper, or the draft can be keyboarded using word processing software on a computer. No matter how you choose to make your rough draft, it's a good idea to skip a line or double space your work. This will give you room to make corrections on pen-and-paper and printed computer drafts, and will also make reading on the computer monitor easier.

The rough draft is **not** the final copy. You may write several drafts before the final one. Don't worry about style and catchy phrases at this point. Instead, follow these basic steps:

**1** Read over your outline, notes, or story map.

**2** Follow your outline or map to write down in sentences the main points of the story.

**3** Write down all your thoughts without stopping to check spelling or grammar, or to edit. Put in as much appropriate information as you can.

**4** Read over your rough draft for obvious mistakes. Change sentences and paragraphs that do not follow logically. Mark corrections in grammar and punctuation (see next page).

**5** Read over the rough draft for style. Consider how you might use some basic tools and techniques (see Terms and Techniques in Writing, pp. 78–82) to add drama or interest to your writing. Fill in details in your paper, or add minor characters, dialogue, or extra episodes to your fiction.

**6** Put the rough draft aside for a while and then read it over again. Is there anything you want to rewrite? Would you like to show it to a friend or family member? Have you made your points clear? Try reading your work aloud to see if it sounds right. Fine-tune your copy.

**7** Prepare a final draft.

> **Skip a space between lines when you write your rough draft. Then you'll have plenty of room to make corrections or additions later.**

# Every Author Needs an Editor
## Editing Sense and Symbols

Every author needs to go over the drafts of his or her writing and edit for sense, flow, and simple errors in grammar and spelling. Following are examples of basic editing symbols and a draft of a paragraph edited to create an improved piece of writing.

> *Growing*
> ~~To grow an~~ orange plac̶e is ~~simple:~~ First save the se̶e̶s from oranges you *nts* *as easy as one: two: three* ⊙ *the next*
> eat. ~~Second,~~ put the seeds ~~in soil in a pot~~ and cover with soil. ~~then water the soil.~~ *Next place* *about one inch apart on top of a container* *e up*
> *inch of additional potting soil, water, and wait.* Keep the pot in the sun and keep watering. According to my mother, You should *Last cover up with about a quarter* *up*
> have oranges in two to t̶r̶ee weeks". *h*

| symbol | meaning | example |
|---|---|---|
| ℓ | delete | I went to the park ~~on Monday.~~ ℓ |
| ∧ | left out, insert | I went to the park. *yesterday* ∧ |
| ∾ | reverse order of letters (transpose) | I went to the park yetsyerday. |
| ◡ | close up, no space | I went to the park ~~on Monday.~~ |
| ≡ | write in capitals | I went to the park on monday. ≡ |
| • • • | stet (let it stand) | I went to the park ~~on Monday.~~ • • • • • |
| ⁋ | start new paragraph | I went to the park on Monday. |
| | | Everyone was there, except Mary. |
| | | She was home with the mumps. |
| | | ⁋ Eric brought a soccer ball. |
| ⊙ | insert period | I went to the park⊙I played on the swings. ∧ |
| ⋏ | insert comma | I went to the park, ate candy and played. ⋏ |
| ⌄ | insert quotation marks | I said, "Wait for me!" |
| ⌄ | insert apostrophe | The parks benches are green. |

# Chapter 3

# Terms and Techniques in Writing

## Alliteration

Repetition of the same sound at the beginning of two or more words that are next to each other or near each other.

> **Fly away, my fine-feathered friend.**
>
> **Drat! I'd deem that a dastardly deed, Duane!**
>
> **A silvery sliver slid from the needle case.**

## Allusion

Something or someone talked about through hints. **Allusions** are often made to people, places, and things that are already well known.

> **The poor dog died this afternoon. Now he is off to the big kennel in the sky. (Big kennel in the sky is heaven.)**
>
> **He's no George Washington. (George Washington means honest person.)**

## Assonance

Vowel rhyme, or words that have the same vowel sound. **Assonance** is often used in poetry.

> **The slowly growing mighty oak did shade our home for years.**

## Cacophony

Noise, or harsh, unpleasant combinations of sounds. *Cacophony* is used in poetry for special effects. It is created by reading onomatopoeic words (see p. 81), or by adding sounds based on the author's instructions, for example, clapping hands, whistling, striking a triangle, etc.

# Characters

The personalities in a story. Most **characters** are people, but sometimes characters are pets, wild animals, or fantasy creatures. The most important character in a book, story, play, or poem is called the **main character**. Other characters are called **secondary**, or **supporting**, **characters**.

In true stories, characters are drawn from real life. The main character in a biography is the person about whom the story is written. The secondary characters are people who have known or have somehow been involved with the life of the main character.

In fictional stories, characters are often good or bad, friendly or mean.

The "good" main character is called the **protagonist** and the "bad" main character is called the **antagonist**. A story can have many antagonists, but usually only one protagonist.

Many fictional characters suffer from a weakness called a **character flaw**. This flaw is important to the action or plot of the story (see Achilles' heel, p. 115) because it is the reason the character gets in trouble or falls into danger.

# Climax

The high point of a story. It is followed by an ending called a **resolution**, or **denouement**.

# Composition

Any written work, either fiction or nonfiction.

# Dialogue

Conversation or talking that takes place between two or more characters. Dialogue is usually enclosed in quotation marks.

# Figure of Speech

A word or phrase used to describe something in an imaginative and usually unrelated way. (See also **allusion**, **imagery**, **metaphor**, and **simile**.)

# Hyperbole

A deliberate exaggeration used as a figure of speech.

**My dog is as big as a ten-ton elephant!**

**Their house was so big, you had to drive a car from the front door to the living room.**

# Imagery

Word painting, or creating imaginary pictures with words. **Imagery** helps readers form pictures in their minds. These pictures make certain points easier to understand and more interesting to read. Such techniques as **allusion**, **metaphor**, and **simile** are examples of imagery.

> **My dog is very happy. (without imagery)**
> **My dog is a pig in mud. (allusion)**
> **The boy would not sit down at his desk. (without imagery)**
> **The boy's desk might as well have been made of pins and needles. (metaphor)**
> **The yellow house was located on the top of a grassy hill. (without imagery)**
> **The house seemed to bloom atop the hill like a daffodil in April. (simile)**

# Metaphor

A comparison of two different things to show a likeness between them that does not use **like** or **as**.

> **The teacher chimed the roll call.**
> **Alice was drowning in tears.**

# Meter

The rhythm made by stressed and unstressed syllables in poetry.

> **There was a crooked man who walked a crooked mile . . .**
> **There once was a penguin named Dave . . .**

*The house bloomed atop the hill.*

# Mood

The feeling of a story, short story, poem, or play. Moods can be happy, sad, scary, tense, gloomy, etc.

# Nonfiction

A piece of writing that tells about people, places, or events that exist, that are happening, or that have existed or happened in the past. Nonfiction can also express an opinion or a true feeling.

# Onomatopoeia

Words that are invented to imitate real sounds. **Bang**, **zip**, **smash**, **rip**, and **grrrrrr** are all examples of onomatopoeia.

# Parable

A story with a moral or religious lesson to be learned. Parables are related to fables.

# Personification

Attributing to things that are not human the personalities and actions of humans. Through personification, Pooh and Paddington behave like human children, not like bear cubs. Feelings can also be personified; for example, **fear grabbed** the victim in its **icy clutches**.

# Plot

The actions or events in a short story, novel, or play.

# Poetry

A feeling or story told in rhythmic verse. Poetry sometimes uses **rhyme** and **imagery**. A work of poetry is called a **poem**. (See also Writing Poetry, p. 88, and Poem Types and Terms, p. 89.)

# Prose

Any writing that is like ordinary speech, unlike poetry.

# Rhyme

The repetition of similar or identical sounds, for example:

| | |
|---|---|
| **red** | **green** |
| **bed** | **bean** |

# Setting

The time and place in which a story, poem, or play takes place. A setting can be a forest, a house, a city, the present, the past, the future, etc.

# Simile

A figure of speech that compares two unlike things. Similes are often confused with **metaphors**. A major difference between similes and metaphors is that a simile is introduced by the words **like** or **as**, and a metaphor is not.

**The lion purred like a kitten.**

**Kim cried as if it were the end of the world.**

# Subject

The **theme**, **topic**, or **main idea** of a sentence, paragraph, or larger piece of writing.

# Theme

The **main idea** or **topic** in a piece of writing.

# Tone

The feeling in a piece of writing, similar to mood. **Tone** or **tone of voice** reflects the feeling of the writer as much as the feeling in the writing. Tone can be nasty, kind, persuasive, angry, friendly, etc.

# Topic

The main idea in a piece of writing.

Chapter **4** # Understanding Other People's Writing

The tools you use to help you write — outlines and story maps — can also be used to help you understand other people's writing. So, too, can Venn diagrams, circle story frameworks, flow charts, time lines, and cause/effect diagrams.

Look at the following story about bats. It's broken down into outline pieces. Compare the pieces to the outline for this story (see pp. 68–69).

Bats
by K.C. Keneally

Wings make bats one-of-a-kind among mammals. They are the only ones that have wings and can fly. Although bats fly more slowly than most birds, they are able to go through much smaller gaps and holes than our feathered friends. When bats aren't flying, they fold their wings along the wing bones and the flesh connects.

Wings aren't the only things that make bats special. They have strange faces that are sometimes really ugly or even scary to look at.

Most bats also have huge ears. They have legs, but no arms. Instead of arms, they have wings.

**I. Bat Bodies**

**IA. Wings**

**IB. Head and Body**

IC. Senses

Bats are mostly blind. Maybe you've heard the expression "blind as a bat"? Instead of seeing with their eyes, bats use echolocation. They send out a high-pitched sound that bounces off food and obstacles like radar. The bounced back sounds are picked up by receptors near the bat's ears.

Bats also sleep upside down.

II. Eating Habits

Most bats eat insects. Some eat mice or even other bats. Still other bats prefer flower nectar or fruits.

III. Life Cycle and Habitat

Bats can live up to 20 years. They are born live, like other mammals, and usually one at a time.

Except for remote islands and extremely cold places, bats are found everywhere in the world. Some bats survive happily in one place all year round. Others have to migrate to find food. In colder climates, bats hibernate during winter months when food is scarce.

Now look at the short story below. See how it can be broken down into the elements of a story map.

**Characters**     **Place**

## Canine Crusaders
### by Kendra Leigh Ealy

**Setting**

**Problem**

"Homer, fetch!" Sally Smith called to her dog. She tossed a Milky Bone toward the backyard fence of her home in Sunnyglade.

The bassett hound ran down the porch step and across the lawn. Then he raised his snout, positioned himself, caught the Milky Bone in his mouth, and plopped down on the spot to enjoy the tasty treat. Just then, a furry black streak flew over the fence and across the grass toward Homer.

"Zoch! Zoch, leave Homer alone!" Sally called after the streak. "I've got a treat for you, too!"

Zoch belonged to the Jeffersons. He and his family had just moved in next door. Zoch and Homer made friends on the spot.

Zoch couldn't have had a better friend than Homer. Everyone around Elm Street—everyone except Mr. Grumpy, of course—loved the sweet-tempered bassett and his constant companion, Sally. So everyone kept a bone or two on hand for their favorite dog. Zoch was quick to understand that Homer was top dog on Elm Street and, by association, he'd be popular, too!

Zoch was hounding Homer less than a week when the mystery of the Milky Bones began. The whole neighborhood was buzzing with the news. No sooner did Sally jump off the school bus than she heard all about it. Everybody's Milky Bones were missing!

Sally ran home, "Mom, where are the bones? Do you know the story? All the dog bones in the neighborhood are gone! Mom, did you hear?"

"Sally, Sally. Calm down," her mother said. "Yes. I've heard the news—but not before our Milky Bones were missing, too."

"Where'd they go, Mom?"

Homer bounded into the kitchen to greet Sally. He was about to leap to her waist and give her a lick, but she didn't open her arms for the greeting. Instead, he cocked his head to listen.

"Well dear, if we knew where the bones were, there wouldn't be a mystery," her mother replied. "The neighbors seem to think Zoch is the culprit, though."

"That's not fair!" Sally cried. "Zoch wouldn't do that!"

"Maybe not, dear, but that's what folks are saying," her mother said.

Sally and Homer moped out the back door and into the yard. No sooner had they hit the lawn than a black streak came flying over the fence.

"Not now, Zorch," Sally scolded. "This is no time for games—and no time for bones, either. You didn't steal the bones, did you, boy?"

Zorch sat near Sally's feet and cocked his head quizzically.

"Of course you didn't, Zorch," Sally answered her own question. "But we've gotta solve this mystery and get you off the hook."

Sally and the dogs walked around the house to Elm Street and turned along Spruce. "Am I imagining it," thought Sally, "or are people giving Zorch dirty looks?" The uncertain feeling grew stronger as she walked with the dogs over to Chestnut and around the corner onto Maple.

Just then, Homer picked up a scent. His hound dog instincts kicked in as he pressed his nose to the ground and slowly inched foward, following the trail of some mysterious odor. Homer was picking up speed, fast on the trail of something—on a canine crusade, Sally thought. Sally and Zorch followed Homer to the end of the block toward Mr. Grumpy's.

"Homer! Stay out of old man Grumpy's yard," she called. Mr. Grumpy was the only neighbor who never had a Milky Bone—or a kind word—for Homer.

But Homer followed the scent right into Mr. Grumpy's yard. Then, suddenly, Zorch bolted toward Mr. Grumpy's, too. Before Sally could stop them, the dogs ran out of sight toward mean Mr. Grumpy's backyard.

By the time Sally reached Grumpy's backyard, Homer was nowhere to be seen. Zorch was stuck under the backyard fence and barking his head off, and old man Grumpy was shouting from his back door.

"Get those vermin dogs outta my yard. I'll call the pound, I'm telling ya! Get those mutts outta here now!" Grumpy's threats were likely to become promises, Sally knew. She had to get Zorch unstuck and find Homer.

Sally knelt by Zorch and stroked his back. Zorch turned his head and gazed at her from the other side of the wire fencing. He took a deep breath and relaxed his muscles. Sally thought he would pull himself back into Grumpy's yard, but Zorch

86

eased himself forward instead. He got clear of the fence and tore off behind Grumpy's toward the vacant lot. Sally chased after him and then Sally stopped, panting. She looked across the vacant lot. It was a great place for hide-n-seek, especially behind all the old tires and junk stashed there. But Sally didn't want to play hide-n-seek now—and she couldn't see Homer or Zorch anywhere.

"Homer, Zorch, come!" Sally hoped the dogs would answer her call. Sure enough, a black lab head popped up from behind an old bedspring in the middle of the lot. Then Homer came bounding into sight. He ran to Sally and took her pant leg in his mouth.

"Homer, stop it," Sally said. "Hey, no nipping."

Homer kept at it, tugging Sally's pant leg and pulling her toward the bedsprings.

"Okay, okay, boy," Sally said. "Are you trying to show me something?"

Sally followed Homer over to the far side of the bedsprings. There among the junk sat Zorch, feasting on Milky Bones— hundreds and hundreds of Milky Bones! But Zorch was not alone. With him was a scruffy dog with a filthy coat and no collar.

"Who are you, little fella?" Sally asked. "Whose doggy are you?"

The scruffy little dog sat back on his haunches and began to growl. But Zorch and Homer must have made some dog signal and their new friend backed off.

"Oh, I get it!" Sally exclaimed. "You're the Milky Bone thief and the Canine Crusaders have sniffed you out!"

"Don't worry, little guy. I'm not interested in your bones," Sally continued. "Now let's go home and tell the neighbors that the case of the missing Milky Bones is solved."

Sally, the crusaders, and Guy (as Sally came to name the scruffy little dog from the vacant lot) went home, steering clear of Mr. Grumpy's house, and frolicking all the way. Sally's dad went over to the lot after dinner with a wheelbarrow. He retrieved the stash of bones Guy had collected and redistributed them among the neighbors. Everyone laughed when they heard the story of the canine crusaders, and everyone came to love the new dogs in the neighborhood—just as much as, but not more than, Homer.

Resolution

87

# Creative Writing

# Chapter 1

# Writing Poetry

## Forms of Poetry

Poems come in many forms. Some rhyme, some don't. Some are long, some short. Some are funny, some are sad. But all poetry has a special rhythm and form that sets it apart from prose or ordinary speech. Two of the most popular poem forms among students are **haiku** and **limerick**.

### HAIKU

A poem written in three lines. The first line is five syllables long, the second seven syllables long, and the last five syllables long. Most haiku is about nature.

**The white herons flew**
**Over the vast blue ocean**
**They fly there no more**

### LIMERICK

A humorous poem written in five lines. The rhyme scheme is a a b b a. The first, second, and last lines each have three strong beats. The third and fourth lines each have two strong beats.

| | |
|---|---|
| A pleasant young teacher from school, | (a) |
| Not inclined to playing the fool, | (a) |
| Tripped on an eraser, | (b) |
| And fell without grace, "Er" | (b) |
| She said, that young teacher from school. | (a) |

# Poem Types and Terms

**Ballad**  A **narrative poem** that tells a story, often a sad one. Ballads, or ballades, have a tricky rhyme scheme. A literary ballad has three eight-line stanzas plus a quatrain at the end.

**Blank verse**  A poem in which the verses have a regular rhythm but do not rhyme.

**Cinquain**  A five-line stanza.

**Couplet**  A pair of lines that share something, usually rhythm and rhyme.

**Elegy**  A sad poem, most often written in honor of a dead person.

**Epic**  A long poem that tells a story, usually based on historic fact, about a hero and his actions. Homer's *Odyssey* is an example.

**Lyric poem**  A short, musical poem that expresses a feeling rather than tells a whole story.

**Narrative poem**  A poem that tells a story. It can be short or long.

**Ode**  A poem, often set to music, that has a theme of nobility or goodness.

**Quatrain**  A four-line stanza.

**Sonnet**  A love poem with a set rhyme scheme, written in 14 lines. Shakespeare wrote many sonnets.

**Stanza**  The paragraph of poetry. A stanza can be two lines long (as in a **couplet**), three lines long (as in a **haiku**), four lines long (as in a **quatrain**), five lines long (as in a **limerick**), or even 14 lines long (as in a **sonnet**). The lines of a stanza share a set pattern, often a set meter, length, and rhyme scheme.

# THE FIRST POETS

No one knows for sure who wrote the first poem. But we do know that ancient holy and wise people called **shamans** and **druids** created **chants**. The chants were rhythmic strings of words used as prayers and spells. Today, chants still stir strong emotions.

Shamans and druids were very powerful people in their societies. They were treated almost as kings and queens. Druids in the Celtic culture were also the keepers of history. Young druids went to school for seven years, learning — by memory — the history of their people from older druids. The history was chanted in verse to help the storyteller remember the story and to keep listeners entertained. In later years, these druids became known as **bards**. A bard is a singer or reciter of poetry.

# Rhyme Schemes

***Rhyme schemes*** are the patterns of rhyming words in poems. Rhyme schemes are written with small letters, beginning with ***a***.

### Couplet

| | |
|---|---|
| **When at last the sun is set** | **(a)** |
| **The fishers will haul in their net.** | **(a)** |

### ABAB

| | |
|---|---|
| **When at last the sun is set** | **(a)** |
| **And the moon is risen above** | **(b)** |
| **The fishers will haul in their net** | **(a)** |
| **And peace will fly in with the dove.** | **(b)** |

### AABB

| | |
|---|---|
| **When at last the sun is set** | **(a)** |
| **And the fishers have hauled in their net** | **(a)** |
| **The moon will rise above** | **(b)** |
| **And peace will fly in with the dove.** | **(b)** |

# Writing a Poem

**1** Choose a topic for your poem.

**2** Choose a form of poetry or create a rhyme scheme and the rhythm. Read over a few of your favorite poems to get started.

**3** Form a picture in your mind to help you express your feelings colorfully and briefly. Write down a few similes or metaphors you may want to use in your poem.

**4** Write a rough draft of your poem. Concentrate on expressing your ideas. You can fix the rhyme scheme and rhythm later.

**5** Check the rhythm and, if necessary, the rhyme scheme. Then rewrite or revise, if necessary.

(See also Rough Draft to Final Copy, p. 76.)

topic

Warts

picture word ideas

– on the skin – ugly
– caused by a virus
– witches and naughty people have warts

rhyme scheme

aabb
or abab

virus / admire us     disease / squeeze / please
presence / essence     slight / blight

rough draft and revisions

                              unpleasant sight
A wart is an ~~ugly old~~ presence.

It looks like my skin has the blight

I know that it comes from a virus.

          I fear                    'cause
But ~~I'm scared~~ it's ~~because~~ witches admire us.

# 2 Writing Prose Stories

## Prose Story Forms

**Prose** stories come in two basic forms: novels and short stories. **Novels** are long stories, with distinct beginnings, middles, and ends. Novels are usually divided into several chapters, and they have characters, setting, and plot. Many novels use dialogue to allow characters to talk to each other. Prose stories are also called **fiction**, something that is made up. Some writers create fiction entirely from their imaginations. Other writers create fiction based on real events or people.

**Short stories** also have beginnings, middles, and ends. They use characters, plot, and setting (see also Story Maps, p. 70).

## Writing a Story

**1** Choose the kind of story you want to write: for example, a mystery, true adventure, romance, science fiction, or horror story. If you are writing a story with a historical setting or one that is based on a true story, be sure you have studied the facts. The more you know the history, the more real your story will seem.

**2** Create a story map. List major characters, a setting, and a theme. Then outline the plot (the most important events) of the story.

**3** Write a rough draft.

# Key Elements of Fiction

Good fiction is the result of the careful crafting of several elements. Among the most important of these elements are:

**Characters**   **the people or main players in a story.**
Characters can be based on people you know or can be entirely made up. Characters must be believable or possess qualities that readers can understand or identify from their own experiences to make them seem real.

**Plot**   **the story line, from beginning to end.**
The plot is the outline of the story's events. A plot can be simple or involve many twists and turns.

**Setting**   **the location of the story.**
The setting is the place (or places) where the action of a story happens.

**Dialogue**   **the words spoken by the character(s) in a story.**
Dialogue is used by many authors — especially by playwrights (see p. 95) — to develop characters, as well as to convey the events of the plot and details of setting.

**Conflict**   **the source of dramatic tension in a story.**
Conflict is used to develop both plot and character(s). The conflict usually drives the plot in a story, and the resolution of the conflict is often the natural ending point of the story.

**Theme**   **the main idea or message of a story.**
The theme of a story is usually described in the answers to one or more of the following questions:

• How did the main character change or what did he or she learn over the course of the story?

• What was the main feeling of the story?

• What idea(s) did the story impart? What was the story about?

• What did the author mean to say in telling the story?

# Just What Kind of Prose Story Is It?
## Glossary of Fiction Forms

Although some stories are difficult to describe, others fit neatly into standard categories:

**Allegory**  A story in which the characters stand for ideas, such as Love, Pride, Greed, or Tolerance. The plot usually has a message or moral about real life.

**Fable**  Like an allegory but short, with fewer characters and a simple moral. Aesop, a writer in ancient Greece, is probably the best-known *fabulist*, or writer of fables.

**Fairy Tale**  An adventure in which the heroes are often royalty or beloved by royalty and the villains are evil witches, sorcerers, or monsters.

**Fantasy**  A tale set in an imaginary world with imaginary characters. For example, animals can talk and fairies roam the countryside in fantasies.

**Historical Fiction**  Stories based on history, with fictional main characters. Historical fiction is sometimes set in real places and includes real people among its characters.

**Horror**  Tales about scary things, from ghosts and goblins to monsters and murderers.

**Informational Fiction**  A story or book that uses fictional characters or settings to tell about real things. For example, a story that explains science experiments might be told by a science teacher working in a fictional lab.

**Legend**  An exaggerated story about a real person or event. For example, there is a story that George Washington, our first president, could never tell a lie.

**Mystery**  Stories in which a problem is created by an unknown element. Mysteries are often crime stories. The main characters in mysteries are frequently detectives searching for a solution.

**Myth**  A story made up to explain real events. Myths help us understand the beliefs and everyday life of the people described in them. Myths once were used to answer difficult questions, such as how the moon and stars came to be, why the seasons change, why the leopard has spots, etc. They also explained the relationships of human beings and gods. Almost every culture in the world has its own set of myths.

**Realistic Fiction**  Stories with imaginary characters and events that are so believable that they could take place in the real world.

**Romance**  Stories in which the main character or characters are looking for love and happiness. Some romances are historical and share many features of historical fiction.

**Science Fiction**  Stories, often set in the future, that use elements of modern science. Some science fiction stories are set on other planets. Others tell of aliens landing on Earth or of computers that run the world.

**Tall Tales**  Humorous stories that are full of exaggeration. Tall tales may or may not be about real people or events.

**True Adventure**  Stories based on real people or real events, but the plot, setting, and characters are partly made up by the author.

# Chapter 3 Writing Plays

## Forms of Plays

A *play* is a story that is meant to be acted out. Like fiction, plays have characters, plots, and settings; beginnings, middles, and ends. The main difference is that, in a play, the story is told in dialogue and through the actions seen on a stage (which are written into the play as stage directions).

**Acts** are like the chapters in a book. In performances, acts are usually separated by breaks called **intermissions**. In plays of more than one act, the first act is called **Act I**, the second act **Act II**, etc. In most plays, acts are divided into **scenes**. Scenes often require changes in time, setting, or characters on the stage. Scenes are numbered with small Roman numerals. The first scene in the second act of a play, for example, is written **Act II**, **scene i**, or **II, i**.

> The author of a play is called a *playwright*. Some plays are short. Short plays are usually performed in one act and are called one-act plays. Longer plays consist of two or three acts.

---

The Day the Ice Cream Truck Broke Down

Act I, scene i: Lights come up to show Jeff and Jamal sitting on a curb, their bikes resting beside them. They are dressed in summer clothes; a cap is backward on Jamal's head. Both boys look hot and tired.

Jeff: Some ride. I could really use a soda! Let's go to my house and get something to drink.

Jamal: I can't move—not even for soda. (Jamal takes off his cap, wipes sweat from his forehead with his other hand, replaces cap.) Gotta rest, Jeff, gotta rest.

# DRAMA: A Brief History

**Greek Drama**

No one knows for certain when drama began. But we do know that more than 2,000 years ago, the Greeks presented powerful dramas that are still performed today.

In Greek theater, all the actors were men. Rather than use makeup, wigs, and costumes, the actors wore masks to fit their characters. Greek dramas also included a group of actors who stood on the side of the stage and chanted their reactions to the story. This group was called the **chorus**.

**Passion Plays**

In the Middle Ages (800–1400), passion plays, dramas about the death of Jesus, were very popular in Europe. In addition to passion plays, other stories from the Bible were acted out, often in the town square on market days.

*Globe Theatre*

**Shakespearean Theater**

By the 1500s, the Bible was no longer the main source for play ideas. Historical plays and dramas about everyday life were also acted out.

Probably the most important playwright of this new era was William Shakespeare (1564–1616). In addition to writing 36 plays, he also built the Globe Theatre at Stratford-upon-Avon in England, the model for theaters ever since.

**Chinese Theater**

The theater in China took shape under the Yuan dynasty (1279–1368). The best-known form of drama today is the Beijing Opera, which became popular at the end of the 18th century. It combines dialogue and songs with dance, symbolic gestures, and acrobatics. The plays are based on Chinese history and folklore.

**Japanese Theater**

Not all dramas are acted out by using dialogue. Japanese Noh drama combines music and movement to tell a story. There is almost no scenery on the stage, and the actors wear masks and often elaborate costumes.

**Other Forms of Drama**

**Mime** is a dramatic form that uses movement and no dialogue to tell a story. **Operas** are dramas in which the characters sing the dialogue rather than speak it. **Musical theater** combines elements of plays with elements of opera so that characters speak and sing their roles. **Puppet theater** uses puppets instead of people to portray the characters in the play.

# Writing a Play

**1** Decide what you want your play to be about.

**2** Create a story map. Choose characters, a setting, and a plot outline. Will your play have one, two, or three acts?

**3** Write a rough draft of your play. Don't worry about the exact dialogue. Instead, write down the action and the main idea, what the characters are saying to each other, and the setting and mood of the story.

**4** When you're pleased with the rough draft, write precise dialogue and stage directions.

**5** Read your play out loud. How does the dialogue sound to you? To a listener?

(See also Rough Draft to Final Copy, p. 76.)

> *Stage directions explain the setting and mood of a scene in a play. They also provide clues as to how the props, sets, and costumes should appear.*

# Scribing a Script:
## Writing Down Dialogue and Stage Directions

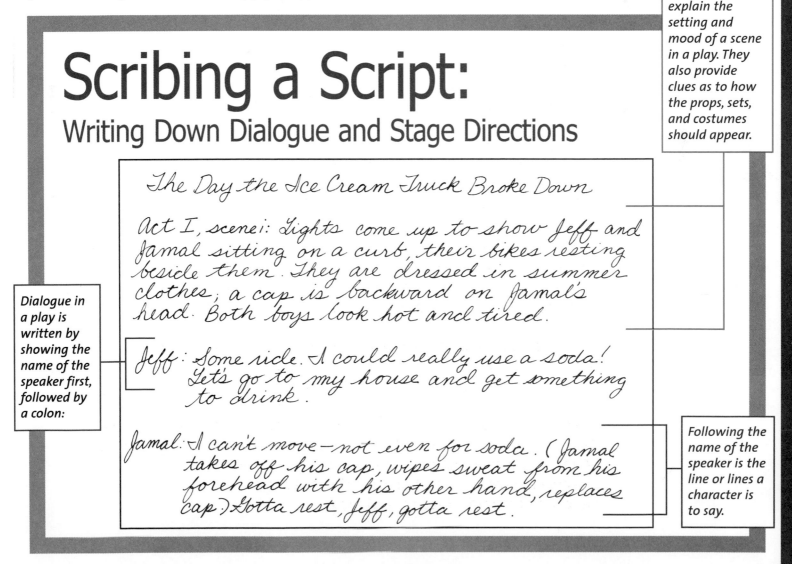

The Day the Ice Cream Truck Broke Down

Act I, scene i: Lights come up to show Jeff and Jamal sitting on a curb, their bikes resting beside them. They are dressed in summer clothes; a cap is backward on Jamal's head. Both boys look hot and tired.

Jeff: Some ride. I could really use a soda! Let's go to my house and get something to drink.

Jamal: I can't move — not even for soda. (Jamal takes off his cap, wipes sweat from his forehead with his other hand, replaces cap.) Gotta rest, Jeff, gotta rest.

> *Dialogue in a play is written by showing the name of the speaker first, followed by a colon:*

> *Following the name of the speaker is the line or lines a character is to say.*

97

# Practical Writing

## Chapter 1 Journals

The word *journal* comes from the Latin word *diurnalis*, which means day. A journal is another name for a *daily diary*, a day-by-day account of events. Some people write in their journals every day, but you may decide to write less often, for example, once a week or whenever you feel you have something important to say.

## Keeping a Journal

**1** Decide if you want to keep a journal in which you write about your feelings and thoughts or one in which you record major events, or both.

**2** Write the date at the top of the page.

**3** Write down the most important things that happened on that day. You might want to explain why you think the events are important.

**4** Every so often, review what you've written in your journal. You may want to continue or expand your thoughts on a particular day, or you may want to note how your thoughts and feelings may have changed.

May 31, 2005

Dear Diary,
    Only two more weeks of school! I can hardly wait for summer vacation – no more pencils, no more books . . .
    Mel and I got in an argument today. It was pretty stupid, but we patched it up. Mr. Hatcher gave us an assignment that included cutting pictures from magazines. I couldn't do it because Mel had my scissors. So I whispered to Mel to give them back. Mr. Hatcher told me to be quiet. Then I raised my hand, but Mr. Hatcher wouldn't call on me. Anyway, I told Mel off at recess and then he got mad. After a while I felt bad. He's more important than scissors!

# 2 Letters

## The ABCs of Letters

Letters come in two basic forms. *Formal*, or *business*, *letters* ask for and provide information. These letters are usually sent to strangers or acquaintances. *Personal letters* are sent between friends and relatives.

## All Letters Have Five Basic Parts

### 1 Heading

A heading includes the date, your address, and, in a formal letter, the name and address of the person to whom you are writing.

### 2 Greeting

A greeting is a quick hello to the person receiving the letter. It usually begins with Dear. Be sure to capitalize the first letter in each word of the greeting. Put a comma at the end of the greeting in a personal letter, a colon in a business letter.

### 3 Body

The body is the main part of the letter. Many people indent the first line of the body. If you indent the first line, then indent the first line of every paragraph in the letter.

### 4 Closing

In a business letter, a closing can be Yours truly, Sincerely, or Regards. In a personal letter, you can write a familiar closing, for example, Your friend, Affectionately, or Love. Be sure to capitalize the first word of the closing and put a comma at the end of the closing.

### 5 Signature

Always sign your letter below the closing. In a formal letter, be sure to print or type your name beneath your signature.

# Writing a Formal Letter

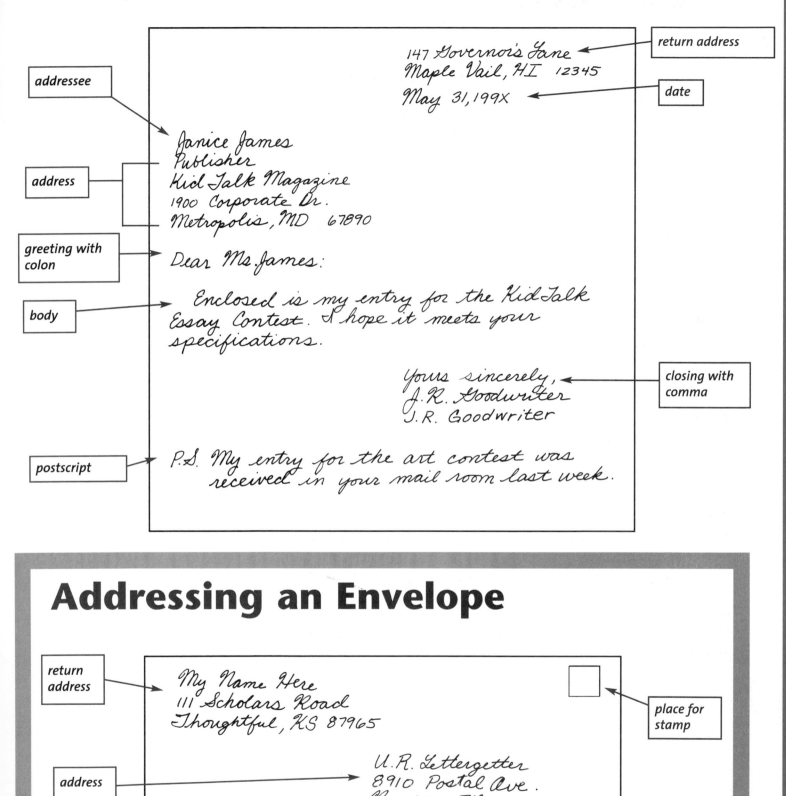

addressee

address

greeting with colon

body

postscript

return address

date

147 Governor's Lane
Maple Vail, HI 12345
May 31, 199X

Janice James
Publisher
Kid Talk Magazine
1900 Corporate Dr.
Metropolis, MD 67890

Dear Ms. James:

Enclosed is my entry for the Kid Talk Essay Contest. I hope it meets your specifications.

Yours sincerely,
J. R. Goodwriter
J. R. Goodwriter

closing with comma

P.S. My entry for the art contest was received in your mail room last week.

# Addressing an Envelope

return address

address

place for stamp

My Name Here
111 Scholars Road
Thoughtful, KS 87965

U. R. Lettergetter
8910 Postal Ave.
Reading, FL 24153

# Writing a Personal Letter

date

*January 1, 2005*

greeting with comma

*Dear Mom,*

body

*Camp is fun—even though the weather's been lousy. I haven't been swimming yet!*

*Tell Bowzer I miss him and remind him I'll be home in 1½ weeks. (Has Bobby been walking him? We have a deal you know!)*

*Love to Aunt Magda and everyone in the neighborhood.*

*Love,*
*Sasha*

closing with comma

# A Party? Writing Invitations

Invitations can be written on sheets of folded paper or on little squares of card stock. They can be formal or casual, colorful or plain. Invitations should always include four pieces of information:

1. **Type of event (birthday party, surprise party, holiday theme party, costume party, club meeting, and so on)**
2. **Time**
3. **Date**
4. **Place**

If you're serving food, you might want to add RSVP to the invitations. RSVP stands for *répondez s'il vous plaît*, and means "please respond." If you add RSVP be sure to supply a phone number or address so invitees will know how to respond.

*Type of Event : Birthday*

*Time : 6:00 PM*

*Date : Saturday, June 10th*

*Place : Susan's house*
*123 Deer Run*

*RSVP : 555·1234*

# Chapter 3 Essays

**Essays** express personal opinions. You can write an essay about any topic or theme that you feel strongly about. Your essay may describe your feelings about the quality of food in the school cafeteria or why you love summer camp. Anything that stirs your emotions is probably a good essay topic.

To write an effective essay, you have to describe your opinions and ideas so that your readers can understand them. It's not enough to say that the food is awful or that camp is terrific. You need to back up your opinion with details so your readers will understand your point of view. You can use argument, humor, or exaggeration to make your points.

> **Essays are made up of four parts:**
> 1. Title
> 2. Introduction
> 3. Body
> 4. Conclusion

## Writing an Essay

**1** Choose a topic.

**2** Outline the major points of your opinion (see Outlines, pp. 68–69).

**3** Write a rough draft of your essay. The introduction should state the topic of your essay and your opinion on the topic. The body should list the reasons you feel as you do about your topic and offer any additional information or experiences to support your opinion. The conclusion should summarize the reasons you listed in the body of your essay and persuade your readers to share your opinion.

> **Be sure to choose an essay topic that's manageable. For example, rather than write about "Sports and Kids," consider writing about "The Pressure on Kids to Win at Sports."**

## What's the Point? Different Types of Essays

Essays can be short or long, serious or witty, based purely in fact or in personal opinion. However, most essays fall into three distinct categories: **expository**, **persuasive**, and **humorous**.

Expository essays explain or describe, and are also called **explanatory** essays and **descriptive** essays.

Persuasive essays are written to convince or persuade readers to adopt the writer's point of view.

Humorous essays can be either expository or persuasive, but use humor to bring home the message.

# Chapter 4

# Reports

**Reports** are factual compositions. They describe the facts about anything — events, places, people, animals, plants, planets, stars, products, and more.

## Writing a Report

**1** Choose a topic.

**2** Gather a variety of resource and reference materials. Be sure you can find enough information to use in your report. If you find too much information, narrow down the subject of your report.

**3** Take notes. As you read through the reference and resource materials, write down the most important information and interesting facts. Be sure to keep track of the information and its sources. You'll need this for the bibliography (see p. 111).

**4** Write an outline (see Outlines, pp. 68–69). Put all the information and interesting facts from your notes into an organized framework.

**5** Write a rough draft. Incorporate as much information as you can from your outline and notes. The introduction should tell the topic of your report. The body should include important information and interesting facts. The conclusion should summarize the main points from the body.

**6** Revise your report. Be sure the information in each of the paragraphs belongs together. Check to see that one paragraph flows smoothly into the next.

(See Rough Draft to Final Copy, p. 76.)

# Research on the Internet

The Internet provides a link to valuable research resources. In order to use the Internet, work through a search engine or portal that allows you to access the World Wide Web.

Most search engines have a "search" command on their home pages (the main screens that appear when you log on to the search engines). Type in a key word or words and click on "search." Once the search is completed, a listing of sources will be provided on the screen.

If too many responses result from your initial search, define your search more narrowly. For example, if you were writing a report on breeds of Siamese cats in your state, you may have to type in "Siamese cats" as your search term. The chances are good that several hundred or more responses would result from your search. Next, try adding a keyword to the search, perhaps, "Siamese cats, Tennessee," and see if you get a more manageable number of resources in response.

If your search produces few or no responses, try to broaden it. For example, if your initial search was defined as "Siamese cats, Palmerston," you might broaden your search by trying "Siamese cats, Tennessee."

Note that good research practice means citing Internet sources just as you would book, magazine, newspaper, or interview sources. Be sure to credit Internet sources by listing Web sites and Internet authors as part of your bibliographies and reference lists (see p. 111).

# Using the Library to Research Your Report

You might have an encyclopedia at home or some books you can use to gather information for a report. But chances are you need to find additional material—so you go to the library. But how do you find the information you need in all those shelves of books? By using the card catalog or computer indexing system. The card catalog or computer index in most libraries is sorted into three categories:

1. **Subject**
2. **Author**
3. **Title**

Within each category, resources are sorted alphabetically. If you know the author of a book or periodical you need for research, use the author index. If you know the title, try the title index. If you don't know the author or the title, you can find information by looking up the subject you're interested in. Just go to the subject index and take a look around.

Some computer indexes allow you to search by keywords that can be typed into a search screen. Use as many keywords as you can to narrow your search for the best sources for your research.

# REVIEWS:
## Cross Between Essay and Report

Reviews combine ingredients of both essays and reports to give the facts — and then express an opinion.

**Book reports** are one kind of review. When you write a book report, you summarize the main events of the story and describe the characters, setting, and plot. You can describe the things you like or dislike about the book, as long as you make it clear that you're stating your opinion.

Reviews are written every day about everything from cars to toys, movies to music. Look in your local newspaper. You'll probably find a review or two.

# NONFICTION: Getting Real

Nonfiction takes on different forms and different topics, depending on the writer and the reasons for writing. Some reports fill entire books or fulfill a particular purpose. These special reports have special names.

| | |
|---|---|
| *Autobiography* | A story of the author's life. |
| *Biography* | A story of a person's life written by another person. |
| *Essay* | A nonfiction story that discusses one topic or theme from a personal point of view  (see p. 103). |
| *History* | An account of a past event or era. |
| *Journal* | A diary or record of day-to-day events  (see p. 98). |
| *News Stories* | Reports written in a special format, usually used in newspapers and magazines  (see p. 109). |
| *Reference* | A collection of useful facts and information organized for quick study rather than for leisurely reading. |
| *Travelogue* | Nonfiction writing, often in the style of a journal or a news story, that tells about a journey or trip to a particular place. |

# Better Book Reports: A Seven-Step Plan

## GETTING STARTED

**1** **Select a book that interests you. Look at the cover.**
Then read the title and the description on the book cover. If the book still seems interesting, open it. Are there pictures? Read a paragraph or two. Are you still interested? If not, try another book.

**2** **Read the book—all of it.**

## GETTING DOWN TO BUSINESS

**3** **Take notes for the first draft of your book report.**
Write down the title, author, and genre (novel, history, biography, and so on) of the book. Then note the names of the major characters and the setting. Next, take notes on the main events, the problem (or conflict) in the book, and its solution. Last, describe one or two favorite episodes from the book.

**4** **Organize your notes and start your first draft.**
Write down the title and author of the story. Then, write a one- to three-paragraph summary of the book. Don't retell every little detail or episode. Instead, limit your summary to the most important events in the story. Next, describe the problem or conflict in the story and how that problem is solved. This is especially important in writing a book report on a novel or piece of fiction. Last, give your opinion of the story and why you feel the way you do.

**5** **Read over your draft.**
Try reading it aloud, and ask a friend or family member to read it, too. Note the parts that you want to revise.

## FINISHING UP

**6** **Edit your book report.**
Reread your edited draft. Are you happy with it? Should you revise it even more, or are you satisfied with your work?

**7** **When you're finished with your draft, write a neat, final copy of your book report.**

## FANCY THOUGHTS

You may want to draw a picture of a scene from the book to include with the report. You might create an illustrated cover or choose to display your book report on a poster with several drawings. Perhaps you'd like to create a filmstrip about the book, one that includes your report and a series of illustrations for each part. Be creative!

# Chapter 5 News Stories

**News stories** are factual stories that usually have a special structure called a **pyramid**. The structure is called a pyramid because the first part of the story tells just the main facts. Then, as the story continues, the facts are described in greater detail to "widen" the story gradually to its "base," or conclusion. A good news story answers the questions **who**, **what**, **when**, **where**, **how**, and sometimes **why**.

**LEAD**
*Tells who, what, when, where, how, and sometimes why*

**DESCRIPTIONS**
*Facts are used to describe the lead and broaden the story into a news pyramid.*

Cowboy Bob Jones attracted attention here Friday when he took 30 sheep to market in his van. He explained that he had become very close to them and wanted their last ride to be comfortable.

The sheep took up every available inch of his van, but Jones said he had no trouble driving with a sheep in his lap.

"They will bring in enough to keep food on the table for a year," he said.

# EXTRA! EXTRA!
## READ ALL ABOUT IT!

Dateline

Headline

Masthead

Photo illustration

Caption

Headline

Cutline

Index

# STUDENT NEWS

Volume 1, No. 1

Mid-November Edition

Unwelcome boosters spotted at pep rally

## Bats Cause Queasy Feelings at Palmerston Pep Rally

Oct. 31. — Bats are living in the Palmerston Elementary gym, according to maintenance engineer I. M. Scarett, who discovered the bats this morning. "There must be 50 or so hanging right behind the stage curtain on the north side of the gym," he reported. Scarett's discovery explains the moving shadows and odd whooshing noises reported in the gym at the evening pep rally on October 28.

Following the rally, student and teacher pep club members asked Palmerston maintenance to investigate the peculiar atmosphere in the gym.

"I sensed an odd presence," 5th grader Sarah Chandler remarked, "and heard kind of a low, beating sound, kind of a 'whoosh, whoosh' sound."

Amar Turk, a 4th grader, added, "The lights were weird. Shadows kept crossing the gym floor. But when I looked up, I didn't see anything. Just more shadows!"

Maintenance director Euby Comfort at first suspected the eerie effects were caused by a problem in the air circulation system. But Scarett, while investigating the air ducts on the gym stage, discovered a more likely culprit.

"Those bats were probably flying around behind the sheer stage curtain the night of the rally," Comfort concluded. Scarett added, "That sure would make one scary shadow play!"

## Presley President

J. R. Presley clobbered the competition in the student council presidential election held last Tuesday, Election Day. Presley won 73 percent of the votes cast by Palmerston Elementary students.

**Longer Lunch**

Presley attributes her landslide victory to her "longer lunch" platform.

"Our lunch period was cut this year from 20 minutes to 15. It's tough to get your lunch from the cafeteria line, take your seat, eat, and bus your tray in that time," Presley said.

In her campaign speech, Presley promised to negotiate with Principal McSwiney to restore the lost five minutes to the lunch schedule for all grades.

110

# Writing a News Story

**1** **Gather facts.**

Be sure you can answer the questions **who**, **what**, **when**, **where**, and **how**. Take notes. If possible, interview people who are involved in the story or who are experts on your subject. Be sure you write down the exact words of the people you plan to quote.

**2** **Write a lead.**

A lead is the first sentence or paragraph in a news story. Think of it as the tip of the pyramid. It tells the basic ideas of the story and gets the reader interested.

**3** **Write the body of the story.**

The body fills in details about the lead.

**4** **Write a headline for your story.**

Try to make the headline a catchy title, one that hints at the action in the news story.

# Credit Where Credit Is Due:
## Writing References and Bibliographies

A **bibliography** shows where you got the information for a report. It is a list of articles, books, or other sources.

Bibliographies are organized alphabetically by the author's last name or, when there is no author named, by the name of the publication. Then the title is listed, followed by the name of the publisher. The place and date of publication are listed at the end.

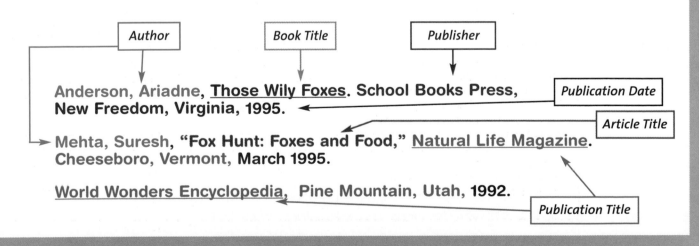

# Chapter 1

# Reading Comprehension

**Reading comprehension**, or how well you understand what you read, is a very important skill for all your school classes, not just English class. So how can you get the most out of your reading and improve your reading comprehension?

Many educators and authors have devised plans to help students improve their reading skills. An approach called **SQR3** is especially popular. SQR3 means

**Survey**
**Question**
**Read**
**Recite**
**Review**

## SURVEY

To survey means to skim through or scan what you are about to read to get a general idea about the material.

## QUESTION

To question means to reason what the author is trying to say in the material. Is the meaning literal? That is, is the author's message conveyed directly in the words he or she uses? Or is the meaning inferential? Does the author say one thing as a symbol for something else?

**The family was in the middle of a raging storm.**

## READ

Once you've surveyed the material and questioned the purpose of the writing, you're ready to read the material word for word. This will reinforce or clarify the impressions gained from your survey and questioning, and will reinforce the details of the story and the author's intention in writing it.

## RECITE

After reading the material, recite in your own words what the author has said in the passage.

## REVIEW

If you have difficulty, reread the material to pick up on the details or ideas that you missed in the first reading.

# 2 Expressions

**Expressions** are words or phrases that are used to convey ideas or feelings beyond their dictionary definitions. Expressions color our thoughts and ideas and provide writers with a shortcut to explaining a complex concept or feeling. Some expressions relate ideas to historical events or people, others to myths, legends, or the Bible.

Many authors use expressions in their books and articles. That means you need to understand the expressions in order to understand their writing.

## Adages, Proverbs, and Maxims

**Adages**, **proverbs**, and **maxims** are sayings that have been used for many years that tell truths about life or human nature. For example:

**A stitch in time saves nine.**

If you sew up a tear when it requires only one stitch to fix, the tear won't get bigger and require a greater effort — nine stitches — to fix later. This expression means that if you pay attention to problems and solve them early, they won't become bigger problems later on.

## Clichés

Clichés are sayings that have been used too much to make a strong impression. Clichés should be avoided in writing and speaking. For example:

**That person is as odd as a three-dollar bill.**

Because there is no such thing as a three-dollar bill, the person is odd or silly.

# Expressions from History, Literature, and the Bible

***Achilles' heel***  A weak spot. In Greek mythology, Achilles was a hero whose only weak spot was on his heel. He was unbeatable in battle until an arrow finally struck him in the heel.

**In school, math was his Achilles' heel.**

***Add insult to injury***  Make a bad situation worse. In a fable by Aesop (see p. 94), a man swats at a fly that has bitten him on his head. Instead of hitting the fly, he hits himself on his sore head. The fly muses that the man has "added insult to injury" by making more pain for himself unnecessarily.

**By insisting he was not stealing when he was caught with the merchandise, John simply added insult to injury.**

***Baker's dozen***  Thirteen, or a little extra. This expression dates back to 1266 in England. Laws were passed by Parliament to protect people from bakers who offered small loaves of bread. To ensure that they met the government standards for weight, the bread bakers threw in an extra loaf per dozen (or 12) sold.

**He gave me a baker's dozen of cupcakes.**

***Cry wolf***  Call for help when there's no danger. About 2,500 years ago, Aesop wrote a story about a shepherd boy who was protecting a flock of sheep from a wolf. The boy was bored and decided to call out as if the wolf were threatening the sheep to see if someone would come. So he cried, "Wolf!"  Sure enough, the village people came running to help the boy protect the sheep. When they discovered the wolf was not around, they were annoyed and returned home. But as the days went by, the boy grew more bored and again cried, "Wolf!" The villagers came again and were even more annoyed when they found the boy was bluffing. They went home. Then one day a wolf really did come. The boy called out, "Wolf! Wolf!" But no one came. The villagers thought he was bluffing. The moral:  If you keep telling lies, no one will believe you, even when you tell the truth!

**He's always crying wolf, so I can't believe he really has a headache.**

***Drop in the bucket***  An amount that doesn't matter. In the Bible, the prophet Isaiah explains that God has created a vast universe. He continues to say that the nations of the world are but drops in the bucket by comparison — unimportant.

**This worksheet is a drop in the bucket compared with the three tests coming up next week!**

***Eat humble pie***  Apologize for making an error. The original expression was to eat **umble** pie. Umble — the heart, liver, and intestines of deer — used to be cooked up in pies for poor people while the wealthy enjoyed the loins and ribs of the animal.

**When she proved I was wrong, I ate humble pie.**

**Go whole hog**  Stop at nothing. Eating pork was against the religious laws of Judaism and Islam, although religious scholars often puzzled over whether it was only certain parts of the hog that could not be eaten. To go whole hog was to forget about the laws and splurge.

**I sure went whole hog when I spent all my allowance on that video game!**

# Idioms

Idioms are sayings whose meanings can't be understood from the individual words in them. For example:

**Apple of one's eye**  The "apple of one's eye" is not an apple in a person's eye. It is a favorite person. The idiom comes from the idea that an apple is a beautiful thing to see and promises to hold good things inside. A favorite person is always pleasant to see and well-loved — that is, good inside.

**Herbert's daughter, Wendy, is the apple of his eye.**

**Greek to me**  Too difficult to understand. In the Shakespeare play *Julius Caesar*, the Romans speak Greek when they want to keep their messages secret. One of the Romans, a fellow named Casca, is asked if he'd heard some important news. He says, ". . . for mine part, it was Greek to me."  Casca had no idea what was said.

**My sister studies algebra, but it's Greek to me.**

**In the doghouse**  In trouble and being punished. In *Peter Pan*, Mr. Darling treats Nana harshly. His children are angry with him, so he sits in Nana's doghouse until they'll speak to him again.

**Dom has been in the doghouse with Mom ever since he left his new bike in the rain.**

**John Hancock**  Your signature. John Hancock was an American patriot and the first signer of the Declaration of Independence. He wrote his name especially large at the bottom of the Declaration to make sure it could be seen.

**They put their John Hancocks on the petition to save the whales.**

**Mad as a hatter**  Crazy. Hatters, or milliners, used mercury to treat the felt fabric used for hats. The mercury gave many of the hatters a severe twitch, which made it impossible for them to work, much less act normally. The Mad Hatter is a well-known character in *Alice's Adventures in Wonderland*.

**Stay away from that guy. He's mad as a hatter.**

**(Open) Pandora's box**  Ask for trouble. In Greek mythology, Pandora was given a box by Zeus, who told her she must never open it because it contained everything bad in the world — illness, sadness, gloom, and misery. But curiosity got the best of Pandora. She opened the box and released all the ills on the world.

*When the principal asked for criticisms, she really opened Pandora's box.*

**Read between the lines**  Guess at the real meaning of things, or the truth behind what is written. Before paper was common, books and official documents were written on parchment made from animal skins. Parchment was very valuable. Rather than throw it away if the messages on it were old, it was reused. The old ink was covered over to make a clear page for another document. On some old parchment, you can actually "read between the lines" because the writing underneath shows through.

*She said the rock star was out of the country, but, if you read between the lines, she probably was just saying that so he wouldn't have to talk to reporters.*

**Slow and steady wins the race**  Aesop's fable "The Tortoise and the Hare" tells about a race between a tortoise and a hare (rabbit). The hare teases the tortoise, but the tortoise keeps going. The hare is so confident that he will win the race that he stops for a nap. As he sleeps, the tortoise, slowly but surely, crosses the finish line first.

*Chonra studied a little every night last week for her social studies test. Kendra crammed the night before. Kendra wrote ten wrong answers, and Chonra wrote only one. Slow and steady wins the race.*

**Sour grapes**  Fools dislike what they cannot have. In Aesop's fable "The Fox and the Grapes," a fox passes a vineyard and spies some tasty-looking grapes. He jumps the fence and tries to grasp the grapes in his jaw, but they are out of reach. The fox tries again and again, but still cannot claim the prized grapes. At last the fox stomps off toward home, saying, "Who needs those grapes? They're probably sour anyway."

*After Ferdie's team lost the soccer match, he said the other team cheated, but I think it was just sour grapes.*

**Wolf in sheep's clothing**  Someone or something that isn't what it appears to be. In one of Aesop's fables, a wolf puts on a sheepskin in order to blend in with a flock of sheep — the easier to kill the sheep for his supper. But the shepherd has the last laugh. He thinks the wolf is a sheep and kills him for his own supper.

*K.C. said she was joining our team because she liked us better, but I'm afraid she may be a wolf in sheep's clothing.*

# FICTION

## ADVENTURE

### The Absolutely True Story: How I Visited Yellowstone Park with the Terrible Rupes
by Willo Davis Roberts
Lewis and Allison didn't realize that going on a trip with the Rupes would be a disaster. Simon & Schuster

### Harry Potter and the Sorcerer's Stone
by J. K. Rowling
The first volume in the adventures of a young wizard and his friends launched a series and became an international sensation and instant classic. Scholastic

### Harry Potter and the Chamber of Secrets
by J. K. Rowling
The next book in the series starts with a bang as a mysterious elf warns Harry that he must never return to Hogwarts School. Scholastic

### Harry Potter and the Prisoner of Azkaban
by J. K. Rowling
In the third book, Harry faces his greatest challenge to date: a confrontation with Sirius Black, an escaped convict and madman . . . or is he? Scholastic

### Harry Potter and the Goblet of Fire
by J. K. Rowling
In the fourth book in the series, the most powerful dark wizard—He-Who-Must-Not-Be-Named—wants Harry! Scholastic

### Holes
by Louis Sachar
In this Newbery-winning novel, Stanley Yelnats is sent to a boys' juvenile detention center in the Texas desert. As punishment, everyday the boys must dig holes, five feet deep and five feet across. Random House

### The Koufax Dilemma
by Steven Schnur
Danny is set to pitch on opening day of the baseball season until he finds out it is the first day of Passover, an important Jewish holiday. Universe

### Secret Letters From 0 to 10
by Susie Morgenstern
Ernest's life is very dull until he meets Victoria.  Puffin

### Slake's Limbo
by Felice Holman
This is the story of a thirteen-year-old boy and how he survives living under New York City's Grand Central Station.  Simon & Schuster

### Spirit Quest
by Susan Sharpe
Aaron and his new friend Robert find adventure on a Spirit Quest, a Native American wilderness experience.  Sagebrush Education

### The Tale of Despereaux: Being the Story of a Mouse, a Princess, Some Soup, and a Spool of Thread
by Kate DiCamillo
This Newbery-winning novel tells the intertwined stories of Despereaux Tilling, a mouse who falls deeply in love with Princess Pea; Chiaroscuro the Rat; and the girl Miggery Sow. Candlewick Press

## FANTASY AND SCIENCE FICTION

### Cougar
by Helen V. Griffith
Nickel has moved to a farm in the country, where he encounters a mysterious horse that helps him deal with a local bully.  HarperCollins

### The Door in the Lake
by Nancy Butts
Joseph disappears while camping. He comes back two years later — with no memory of his time away.  Puffin

### The Giver
by Lois Lowry
Given his lifetime assignment in the Ceremony of Twelve, Jonas becomes the receiver of memories shared by only one other in his community and learns the terrible truth about the society in which he lives.  (Newbery Medal) Houghton

### Harry the Poisonous Centipede
by Lynne Reid Banks
Harry follows his best friends into the dangerous land of HOO-MINS.  Avon

### Help! I'm Trapped in Obedience School
by Todd Strasser
Jack accidentally turns his best friend into a dog.  Scholastic

### It's All Greek to Me
by Jon Sciezka
As they are about to go on stage, Joe, Fred, and Sam are transported back to the time of Zeus and the other gods in Greek mythology, who, strangely enough, behave much as the characters in the trio's class play.  Puffin

### King of Shadows
by Susan Cooper
While working in a replica of the famous Globe Theater in London, Nat finds himself transported back to 1599 and performing in the original theater under the guidance of Shakespeare himself.  Simon & Schuster

### The Lost Flower Children
by Janet Taylor Lisle
Olivia and Nellie find wonder and hope in their great-aunt's garden, which is filled with fabulous characters and deep emotions.  Putnam

### Monster of the Month Club
by Dian Curtis Regan
Rilla thinks her stuffed monsters are cute—until they start to wake up!  Scholastic

### Mrs. Frisby and the Rats of NIMH
by Robert C. O'Brien
An intriguing story about a race of superrats created by the scientists at NIMH.  Aladdin

### My Life Among the Aliens
by Gail Gauthier
Two brothers begin to wonder if their mother's unusual cooking is attracting the aliens who keep showing up at their house.  Putnam

### Nosepickers from Outer Space
by Gordon Korman
Fourth-grader Devin's disappointment in the nerdy live-in exchange student changes to amazement when he realizes that the "nerd" is an alien who communicates home through his nose!  Disney Press

### The Phantom Tollbooth
by Norton Juster
Milo embarks on an exciting adventure in a strange country of edible words and mysterious creatures, fabulous wit and wordplay.  Random House

### Skellig
by David Almond
Unhappy about his baby sister's illness and his move into a dilapidated old house, Michael retreats to the backyard shed, where he discovers a strange, owl-like man.  Random House

### The Trolls
by Polly Horvath
Aunt Sally tells stories about strange relatives and trolls.  Farrar, Straus & Giroux

### The World's Worst Fairy Godmother
by Bruce Coville
Why is Maybelle considered the world's worst fairy godmother? Maybe it's her secret enemy. . . .  Simon & Schuster

# HISTORICAL FICTION

### Bandit's Moon
by Sid Fleischman
Annyrose, a twelve-year-old girl disguised as a boy, recaps the adventures of Joaquin Murieta and his band of outlaws.  Random House

### Catherine, Called Birdy
by Karen Cushman
The thirteen-year-old daughter of an English country knight records her struggle to escape the usual role of women in her time and place.  HarperCollins

### Crispin: The Cross of Lead
by Avi
This Newbery-winning novel transports readers back to fourteenth-century England, where a young serf on the run from his miserable past comes to discover not only his true identity but also a sense of self-worth.  Hyperion

### Hero Over Here: A Story of World War I
by Kathleen V. Kudlinski
A young boy is left behind while his father and older brother fly in World War I. His disappointment turns to pride when he is able to support the war effort on the home front. Viking

### Journey to Nowhere
by Mary Jane Auch
In 1815, Mem's family moves from Connecticut to the wilderness of western New York. Bantam Doubleday Dell

### The Keeping Room
by Anna Myers
Left in charge of his family during the Revolutionary War, thirteen-year-old Joey's view of what is right and wrong changes. Will his father feel betrayed? Puffin

### A Long Way from Chicago
by Richard Peck
A boy recounts his annual summer trips to rural Illinois with his sister during the Great Depression. The kids visit their larger-than-life grandmother.  Puffin

### Love from Your Friend, Hannah
by Mindy Warshaw Skolsky
It is 1937. Hannah's best friend has moved away and she is looking for a pen pal. HarperCollins

### The Midwife's Apprentice
by Karen Cushman
This Newbery-winning novel is set in medieval England, where a nameless and homeless girl is sheltered by a sharp-tempered midwife and, in spite of obstacles and great hardship, finds a place in the world.  Clarion

### Number the Stars
by Lois Lowry
In 1943, during the German occupation of Denmark, ten-year-old Annemarie learns how to be brave when she helps shelter her Jewish friends from the Nazis. (Newbery Medal)  Bantam

### Out of the Dust
by Karen Hesse
In a series of poems, fifteen-year-old Billie Jo relates the hardships of living on her family's wheat farm in Oklahoma during the Depression's dust bowl years. (Newbery Medal)  Scholastic

### A Single Shard
by Linda Sue Park
This is a tender tale of a twelfth-century Korean boy named Tree-ear who must overcome a host of obstacles in order to attain his life's dream. (Newbery Medal)  Random House

### Walk Two Moons
by Sharon Creech
After her mother leaves home suddenly, thirteen-year-old Sal and her eccentric grandparents take a car trip retracing her mother's route. Along the way, Sal entertains her grandparents with the story of her friend Phoebe. (Newbery Medal)  HarperCollins

### The Well: David's Story
by Mildred D. Taylor
The Longmans' generous act of sharing their well water with both white and black neighbors sparks danger and brings tension to the town.  Puffin

### A Year Down Yonder
by Richard Peck
This Newbery-winning novel is set in 1937 in a tiny Illinois town. Told through the eyes of fifteen-year-old Mary Alice, this book is loaded with laughs as well as life lessons.  Puffin

# MYSTERY

### Christie & Company: In the Year of the Dragon
by Katherine Hall Page
Christie and her friends try to solve a mystery during the Chinese New Year celebration.  Avon

### Going Through the Gate
by Janet Anderson
In a small town, five sixth-grade students prepare for their teacher's mysterious annual graduation ceremony.  Sagebrush Education

### How Can I Be a Detective If I Have to Baby-sit? (Vol. 2)
by Linda Bailey
Stevie thinks she has better things to do—like catch a smuggler—than watch a three-year-old.  Albert Whitman

### I Dream of Murder
by Catherine Dexter
Jere doesn't know if his dream is a nightmare or a warning of the future.  William Morrow

### Journey into Terror
by Bill Wallace
Before taking off for Oklahoma to see his father and his new family, Samuel Ross accidentally takes a picture that he shouldn't have. Now people are after him!  Simon & Schuster

### Night of the Chupacabras
by Marie G. Lee
Lupe and her friends don't believe in bloodsucking creatures, but something is trying to change their mind.  William Morrow

### Orp and the FBI
by Suzy Kline
A mysterious intruder, a strange letter, and a vacant house combine to make an exciting mystery for twelve-year-old Orp.  Penguin

### Running Out of Time
by Margaret Peterson Haddix
When a diphtheria epidemic hits her 1840s village, thirteen-year-old Jessie discovers that her "village" is actually a 1996 tourist site under observation by heartless scientists.  Simon & Schuster

### Sammy Keyes and the Hotel Thief
by Wendelin Van Draanen
Thirteen-year-old Sammy's urge to speak her mind gets her in trouble when she involves herself in the investigation of a robbery at the run-down hotel across the street from the seniors' building where she lives with her grandmother.  Random House

### Sebastian (Super Sleuth) and the Flying Elephant
by Mary Blount Christian
When Detective John Quincy Jones is told to find the circus's missing elephant by nightfall, his faithful canine companion must come to his rescue as usual. Macmillan

### The Wreckers
by Iain Lawrence
Off the coast of England in 1799, shipwrecked fourteen-year-old John attempts to save his father and himself while dealing with an evil secret  surrounding the village where he  is stranded.  Bantam Doubleday Dell

## REALISTIC FICTION

### Because of Winn-Dixie
by Kate DiCamillo
Because of Winn-Dixie, a big, unhappy, and ugly dog, ten-year-old Opal learns ten things about her long-gone mother from her preacher father. Opal begins to find her place in the world and let go of some of her sadness.  Candlewick Press

### Bud, Not Buddy
by Christopher Paul Curtis
Times are tough in Flint, Michigan, in 1936, but ten-year-old Bud escapes a bad foster home and sets out in search of the man he believes is his true father—the famous band leader H. E. Calloway of Grand Rapids. (Newbery Medal) Random House

### Carolina Crow Girl
by Valerie Hobbs
A crow brings a poor girl and a rich boy together. Farrar, Straus & Giroux

### Crash
by Jerry Spinelli
Through his relationship with an unusual Quaker boy and his love for his ill grandfather, tough seventh-grader Crash learns the true meaning of friendship and the importance of family. Knopf

### Fourth Grade Rats
by Jerry Spinelli
Suds learns that his best friend is wrong: You don't have to be a tough guy, a "rat," to be a grown-up fourth grader. Scholastic

### Frances Dances
by Ilene Cooper
Frances can't wait for the dance studio to open in her town, but will she have the courage to perform in the recital even if her best friends drop out? Knopf

### Frindle
by Andrew Clements
When fifth-grader Nick Allen invents a new word, he starts a chain of events that quickly gets beyond his control. Simon & Schuster

### Joey Pigza Swallowed the Key
by Jack Gantos
Joey is faced with placement in special education classes unless he shapes up. HarperCollins

### Just Juice
by Karen Hesse
It is up to nine-year-old Juice to help her father save their house by returning to school and learning how to read. Scholastic

### Keep Ms. Sugarman in the Fourth Grade
by Elizabeth Levy
Jack's brief introduction to self-esteem by Ms. Sugarman is shattered when the teacher is promoted to principal in the middle of the year. HarperCollins

### A Llama in the Family
by Johanna Hurwitz
Sure that his birthday present will have two wheels and pedals, Adam is far from delighted when it turns out to have fur, four legs . . . and spits! William Morrow

### Meet Calliope Day
by Charles Haddad
Determined to get back the pink fangs her teacher took from her, nine-year-old Calliope first needs to win over the woman next door. Sagebrush Education

### Navajo Summer
by Jennifer Owings Dewey
Jamie tries to escape her parents' divorce by running away to her Navajo friends.
Sagebrush Education

### Nerd No More
by Kristine L. Franklin
Wiggie is rejected after his mom stars in an educational science show.  Candlewick Press

### Sun & Spoon
by Kevin Hankes
After the death of his grandmother, ten-year-old Spoon tries to find the perfect keepsake to help him remember her.  Puffin

### Thank You, Mr. Falker
by Patricia Polacco
It is not until the fifth grade, when a new teacher arrives, that Tricia comes to understand and overcome her reading problem.  Philomel

### The View from Saturday
by E. L. Konigsburg
Four students, each with his or her own individual stories, develop a close bond and attract the attention of their teacher, a paraplegic, who chooses them to represent their sixth-grade class at the Academic Bowl competition.  (Newbery Medal) Simon & Schuster

### Wander
by Susan Hart Lindquist
Grieving for their dead mother, twelve-year-old James and his younger sister, Sary, find healing in their affection for a stray dog.  Sagebrush Education

### White Water
by P. J. Petersen
A young boy learns how to face his fears and find his courage on a white-water rafting trip with his adventure-loving father.  Random House

### Woodsie
by Bruce Brooks
At the start of the new ice hockey season, Woodsie alone believes that his teammates can pick themselves up after several key players defect to a rival team.
HarperCollins

### Would My Fortune Cookie Lie?
by Stella Pevsner
Alexis doesn't know which is her bigger problem—moving or someone following her.
Simon & Schuster

### Zucchini Out West
by Barbara Dana
Billy learns that Zucchini might be an endangered ferret, so the creature can't be kept as a pet. HarperCollins

# NONFICTION

## BIOGRAPHY/AUTOBIOGRAPHY

### The Abracadabra Kid: A Writer's Life
by Sid Fleischman
The Newbery-winning children's book writer recounts how he set out from childhood determined to be a magician. William Morrow

### Basher Five-Two: The True Story of F-16 Fighter Pilot Captain Scott O'Grady
by Scott O'Grady
An F-16 fighter pilot tells his story. Bantam Doubleday Dell

### Bull's-Eye: A Photobiography of Annie Oakley
by Sue Macy
National Geographic Society

### Bully for You, Teddy Roosevelt
by Jean Fritz
This lively biography captures the exuberance and enthusiasm of president, conservationist, explorer, and author Theodore Roosevelt. Putnam

### Childtimes: A Three-Generation Memoir
by Eloise Greenfield and Lessie Jones Little
In this lyrical memoir, three African-American women—a grandmother, daughter, and granddaughter—recreate their childhoods. HarperCollins

### Christopher Reeve: Actor and Activist
by Margaret L. Finn
The life of the actor before and after his horseback riding accident. Chelsea House

### Colin Powell: A Biography
by Jim Haskins
This biography traces the life of Colin Powell, the first African-American Chairman of the Joint Chiefs of Staff and the man who oversaw Operation Desert Storm. Scholastic

### Confucius: The Golden Rule
by Russell Freedman
Newbery-winner Freedman delves deep into Chinese history in this intelligent and fun biography. Scholastic

### The Double Life of Pocahontas
by Jean Fritz
A biography of the famous Native American princess, emphasizing her relationship with John Smith and the roles she played in two very different cultures. Putnam

### Facing the Lion: Growing Up Maasai on the African Savanna
by Joseph Lemasolai Lekuton
This autobiography describes the author's extraordinary passage between cultures and his continuing effort to hold the two in balance. National Geographic Society

### The First Woman Doctor

by Rachel Baker

This is an engrossing biography of Elizabeth Blackwell, the first female doctor, who also established a women's hospital and medical college. Scholastic

### Four Perfect Pebbles: A Holocaust Story

by Lila Perl

Marion and her family try to escape the Holocaust. HarperCollins

### Frederick Douglass Fights for Freedom

by Margaret Davidson

Born a slave, Frederick Douglass went on to become one of the most famous freedom fighters in modern times. Scholastic

### Gertrude Chandler Warner and the Boxcar Children

by Mary Ellen Ellsworth

This biography traces the life and times of the woman who created the Boxcar Children series of books. Albert Whitman

### How I Came to be a Writer

by Phyllis Reynolds Naylor

In her autobiography, Newbery-winner Naylor details her career from grade school to the present. Simon & Schuster

### Indian Chiefs

by Russell Freedman

Compelling profiles of six Native American chiefs who led their people through a historic crisis. The book includes photographs and a map. Holiday House

### It Came from Ohio! My Life as a Writer

by R. L. Stine

R. L. Stine tells many of his "secrets" of how he became a writer and where he gets some of his ideas. Econo-Clad

### Knots in My Yo-yo String: The Autobiography of a Kid

by Jerry Spinelli

The Newbery-winning children's author presents a humorous account of his childhood and youth in Norristown, Pennsylvania. Knopf

### Leon's Story

by Leon Walter Tillage

The son of a North Carolina sharecropper recalls the hard times his family and other African Americans faced in the first half of the twentieth century, and the changes the civil rights movement helped bring about. Farrar, Straus & Giroux

### Looking Back: A Book of Memories

by Lois Lowry

Using family photographs and quotes from her books, the Newbery-winning author provides glimpses into her life. Houghton Mifflin

### Lost Star: The Story of Amelia Earhart

by Patricia Lauber

A fascinating look at America's most famous female aviator. Scholastic

### Michelle Kwan: My Special Moments
by Michelle Kwan
The award-winning ice skater traces her life from childhood to the Olympics. Hyperion

### My Life in Dog Years
by Gary Paulsen
The author describes some of the dogs that have had special places in his life, including Dirk, who protected him from bullies, and Cookie, who saved his life. Bantam Doubleday Dell

### Nelson Mandela: "No Easy Walk to Freedom"
by Barry Denenberg
The story of Mandela's remarkable life, from his boyhood to his twenty-six-year imprisonment to his release and visit to the United States. Scholastic

### On the Course with . . . Tiger Woods
by Matt Christopher
This biography examines the life and athletic career of the popular young golfer who won the Masters Tournament in 1997. Little Brown

### On the Court with . . . Michael Jordan
by Matt Christopher
This biography examines the life and basketball career of the high-scoring player for the Chicago Bulls. Little Brown

### Pride of Puerto Rico: The Life of Roberto Clemente
by Paul Robert Walker
This biography traces the life of the baseball superstar who was noted for his achievements on and off the baseball field before his untimely death in an airplane crash. Harcourt

### The Tarantula in My Purse: and 172 Other Wild Pets
by Jean Craighead George
A collection of autobiographical stories about the author's life, family, and many wild pets. HarperCollins

### Through My Eyes
by Ruby Bridges
Ruby remembers being the first child to integrate the New Orleans school system in 1960. Scholastic

## INFORMATIONAL BOOKS

### Children of the Wild West
by Russell Freedman
Historical photographs and explanatory text present a picture of life in the American West from 1840 to the early 1900s. Houghton Mifflin

### Eleanor Roosevelt: A Life of Discovery
by Russell Freedman
A photo-essay of the first wife of a president to have a public life and career of her own. Houghton Mifflin

### Exploring the Titanic
by Robert D. Ballard

This book describes the luxury liner that sank in 1912 and the subsequent discovery and exploration of its underwater wreckage. Scholastic

### Fields of Fury: The American Civil War
by James M. McPherson

Atheneum

### Fire in Their Eyes: Wildfires and the People Who Fight Them
by Karen Magnuson Beil

The ferocity of fire is forcefully depicted in both text and photographs. Harcourt

### Great Fire
by Jim Murphy

Told through the eyes of several survivors, this is a fascinating account of the infamous fire that destroyed most of Chicago in 1871. Scholastic

### Immigrant Kids
by Russell Freedman

During the late 1800s and early 1900s, immigrant kids sold newspapers, hauled firewood, worked in sweatshops, and did many other kinds of labor. After work, they played, fought rivals, and became part of the fabric of American life. Puffin

### In Defense of Liberty: The Story of America's Bill of Rights
by Russell Freedman

Discover the origins, applications, and challenges to the Bill of Rights, the ten amendments to the U. S. Constitution. Holiday House

### Island of Hope: The Story of Ellis Island and the Journey to America
by Martin W. Sandler

Scholastic

### Kids at Work: Lewis Hine and the Crusade Against Child Labor
by Russell Freedman

Using the photographs of Lewis Hine, an early-twentieth-century photographer and schoolteacher, Freedman shows the horrifying effects of child labor. Hine's devastating photographs convinced Americans that Congress had to pass child labor laws. Houghton Mifflin

### Lincoln: A Photobiography
by Russell Freedman

The Newbery Medal book traces Lincoln's boyhood, marriage, young professional life, and presidency. Clarion

### Martha Graham: A Dancer's Life
by Russell Freedman

In words and pictures, the author recounts the life of the American dancer, teacher, and choreographer who became a leading figure in modern dance. Clarion

### Prairie Visions: The Life and Times of Solomon Butcher

by Pam Conrad

You can experience the lives of Nebraska pioneers at the turn of the century through the eyes and photographs of a man named Solomon Butcher. Econo-Clad

### Shipwreck at the Bottom of the World: The Extraordinary True Story of Shackelton and the Endurance

by Jennifer Armstrong

An exciting and fascinating account of the 1914 expedition that left Shackelton and his men shipwrecked on the frozen Antarctic Sea.  Crown

### The Top of the World: Climbing Mount Everest

by Steve Jenkins

Beautifully illustrated with cut-paper collage, this book delves into the story of the history, geography, climate, and dangers of the world's tallest mountain. Houghton Mifflin

### Tornadoes

by Seymour Simon

The author describes the location, nature, development, and destructive effects of tornadoes, as well as how to stay out of danger.  HarperCollins

### Volcano: The Eruption and Healing of Mount St. Helens

by Patricia Lauber

An engaging account of how and why Mount St. Helens erupted in 1980 and the destruction it caused. The book also explores how life has returned to the area. Simon & Schuster

### Weather

by Seymour Simon

The author describes the causes of weather and its changing patterns. There is also a section on forecasting weather.  HarperCollins

### Who Really Discovered America?

by Stephen Krensky

This humorous, informative book describes the arrivals in America of Columbus's predecessors, from the Vikings to Asian nomads crossing a land bridge.
Hastings House Daytrips

### Who Really Discovered America? Unraveling the Mystery and Solving the Puzzle

by Avery Hart

This book not only questions theories about America's discovery but also encourages readers to keep an open mind and think for themselves. Ideals Publication

### Working With Wildlife: A Guide to Careers in the Animal World

by Thane Maynard

Many students dream of working with wildlife, but don't know how to go about making their dreams come true. This informational guide provides answers, focusing on both common and uncommon careers with animals.  Scholastic

### The Wright Brothers: How They Invented the Airplane

by Russell Freedman

This book explores the lives and achievements of Orville and Wilbur Wright. Their achievements are documented in photographs as well as words. Holiday House

# Index